T0274180

Praise for *Coffee's for Closers*

'What Tony Morris does not know about sales, quite frankly, isn't worth knowing. He's such a fantastic guy too'.

—Richard McCann,
Times No. 1 Bestselling Author
and Founder of the iCan Academy.

'*Coffee's for Closers* is the most authentic and real sales book out there and is a must-read for anyone working in sales. Real tactics, real tips and real strategies from one of the best sales trainers in the world. If you want to sell more, buy this book, read it and apply it'.

—Dan Disney

ROCK SOLID! Tony Morris' *Coffee's for Closers* is completely oozing with fantastic tips, tricks and outstanding guidance on how to succeed in every aspect of the selling process in a surprisingly compact format. You'll get a full return on your investment by the second chapter. Highly recommended!

—James Muir,
CEO of Best Practice International
and Bestselling Author of *The Perfect Close*

'One thing that strikes me about Tony's words in this book is the stories he tells. Because he tells them as they are, it allows me to see myself in those stories and, of course, any seller worth their weight has travelled the same path. Great read'.

—Bernadette McClelland,
Sales Leadership and StorySeller Expert

'Having met Tony on his podcast, his energy, knowledge and charisma are what makes him a force to be reckoned with'.

—Daniel Priestley

'True top sales professionals are always adding to their bank of knowledge, and *Coffee is for Closers* should be part of that library. Tony delivers all meat, and no fluff or theory. . .page after page, how-to- after how-to of solid, instantly usable sales gold in his conversational, speaking-from-experience, entertaining style. Get your highlighter and notebook ready as you will be pulling lots of 'I need to do this' tips from the book. Get it today'.

—Art Sobczak,
Author of *Smart Calling: Eliminate the Fear, Failure, and Rejection from Cold Calling*

Coffee's for Closers is a comprehensive sales guide that presents actionable strategies that you can immediately put into practice. Read it with a highlighter handy. You'll need it!

—Lee B. Salz,
Bestselling Author of *Sell Different!*
and *Sales Differentiation*

Tony has a unique way about him; he exceeds expectations and does what he says he will do. A fine quality in life and business, and a rarity, in my experience, amongst salespeople. Furthermore, his book is a perfect reflection of the man himself. He is a real character, hard-working, resourceful, ambitious and very funny, and those traits jump out from every page. He tracks his career from a painful start, full of setbacks, matched only by an obstinate passion to succeed and learn from his mistakes. He shares his business experiences, successes and early failures, the lessons he has learned each time, and the techniques he employs to circumvent roadblocks, create opportunities and improve his 'strike rate'.

—Claude Littner,
Entrepreneur, Trouble Shooter
and star of the show *The Apprentice*

Coffee's for Closers

Coffee's for Closers

The Best Real-Life Sales Book You'll Ever Read

Tony Morris

This edition first published 2023

Copyright © 2023 by Tony Morris

Edition History

Published by New generation Publishing in 2012. Copyright © Tony Morris 2012.

Registered Offices
John Wiley & Sons, Inc., 111 River Street, Hoboken, NJ 07030, USA
John Wiley & Sons Ltd, The Atrium, Southern Gate, Chichester, West Sussex, PO19 8SQ, UK

Editorial Office
The Atrium, Southern Gate, Chichester, West Sussex, PO19 8SQ, UK

For details of our global editorial offices, customer services, and more information about Wiley products visit us at www.wiley.com.

Library of Congress Cataloging-in-Publication Data is Available:

ISBN 9780857089557 (Hardback)
ISBN 9780857089618 (ePDF)
ISBN 9780857089625 (ePub)

Cover Design: Wiley
Cover Image: © kyoshino/Getty Images

SKY10045614_041423

This book is dedicated to my late Dad, Ray, for being my inspiration, for teaching me right from wrong and showing me how to be the best salesperson in the world by just being me.

I would like to thank my gorgeous wife, Shana, for being a continuous support to me and spurring me on every day to succeed. Most importantly, for giving me the best gift in the world, my adorable children, Harry and Poppy. The three of you are my entire world and every day when I think about you all, it quickly reminds me why I work as hard as I do. I am truly blessed!

A big thank you to my father-in-law. You brought into the world the greatest gift I had ever imagined, my beautiful wife Shana.

And I must mention my amazing mum, Ros, and my late mother-in-law, Tina. I love you both dearly.

A special mention to Shana's great late Uncle Ken. He spent hours upon hours with me writing the first edition of Coffee's for Closers *in 2012, and I am so grateful to him.*

Contents

Contents

Contents

Contents

Contents

Foreword

'*Put that coffee down! Coffee is for closers only*'.
Alec Baldwin delivered this iconic line in one of the greatest 'sales' movie scenes ever shown on the big screen.

I admit that I've watched this scene so many times that I can repeat the entire dialogue by heart. I'm not alone. Over the past 30 years, since the movie *Glengarry Glen Ross* was released, legions of sales professionals have done the same.

'*The leads are weak*'.

'*You're weak!*'

Top sales professionals, the ones I call ultra-high performers, lean into this scene. They love the raw, unveiled truth about what it takes to make it in one of the world's toughest professions.

'*First prize is a Cadillac Eldorado. Second prize, a set of steak knives. Third prize is you're fired*'.

The highest-earning sales professionals, the same ones that make more money than doctors, lawyers, engineers, architects and other high-earning professionals, love this line because it cuts right to the quick, putting the truth on the table – the game of sales, at the core, is a raw, Darwinian survival of the fittest.

In sales, you write your own destiny. Income and success are in direct correlation to talent, skills, mindset and effort. This, by the way, is why the rewards always go to those who can make it rain.

But, selling is hard. In sales, there are no shortcuts. No easy buttons. No excuses. You either deliver results or you will be fired. In this profession, you are not judged by what you have sold, but rather what you produce today.

Miss quota and you are out. Exceed quota and you are a hero. You cannot kumbaya your way around this brutal truth. The pressure to sell and the demand to perform are unrelenting. Salespeople have the most lucrative jobs in business because most people wouldn't last a minute in your shoes.

This is exactly why I am so excited to introduce this new book from my good friend Tony Morris. I love Tony because he loves the sales profession the same way I do. His is an authentic, visceral love that drives his passion to help sales professionals reach peak performance.

Coffee's for Closers is a wonderful book. It's packed with fantastic stories, truths and humour. Tony's back-to-the-basic lessons will help you hone your sales skills, build mental resilience and spark the internal drive and relentless persistence that are at the heart of sales success.

Read this book. Devour this book. Then read it again. Tony will teach you how to perform at your peak, deliver when the game is on the line, and earn that cup of coffee.

Gandhi said, 'We should live as if we will die tomorrow and learn as if we will live forever'. When you make the commitment to learn, you'll be happier, more motivated and maximize your income.

Jeb Blount, CEO of Sales Gravy
and author of *Fanatical Prospecting*

Preface

After reading over 260 sales books and listening to over a hundred on Audible, it became frustratingly apparent that there were no answers to everyday sales challenges. There were some good techniques and interesting ideas; however, I personally struggled to put them into practice in my everyday life as a salesman.

I have learned so much from the sales gurus, like Brian Tracey, Zig Ziglar and Jim Rohn, yet always struggled to put things into practice in my actual sales role. I have seen the most incredible motivational speakers in the world, like Anthony Robbins; he talks at great length about how he was penniless in his teens and by his mid-twenties he made his first million. To some degree, this is incredibly inspirational and allows your mind to wander and gives you the hope and belief that anything is possible. On the flipside comes the frustration and unanswered questions on 'how is it possible?' The latter part is never really divulged – not in detail anyway.

This is where the motivation for my book was born. I wanted to write a book that not only shares lots of innovative and easy-to-understand techniques but also it was imperative that these could be implemented into a sales professional's daily role. I am not a millionaire, yet, although I am on my way to becoming one. I do not have a single doubt that I will achieve this and more, and I hope that doesn't come across as arrogant.

The reason for my confidence and belief is that at the age of 21, when I had been in sales for a couple of years, the thought of earning a six-figure salary seemed like a dream. The thought of writing a sales book did not even cross my mind, as I would have immediately dismissed it as ludicrous. If someone told me I'd be able to afford a four-bedroom house, drive a lovely sports car and buy my wife her dream car, I would have imagined I'd chosen six lucky numbers. However, I have achieved all of the above, and I like to think that I am a good husband and dad, which has cemented my beliefs that if you put your mind to it and work really hard, you can achieve what you want.

I have made numerous mistakes along the way and I know I have many more to come. I have developed my knowledge and abilities on the back of these failings. In a bizarre way, I am looking forward to my inevitable errors as there are no greater lessons. My dad used to say to me, 'What you put in is what you get out', and I never stopped believing this for a second. I graft harder than ever before and always give it my all. When you start to see wonderful things happening around you, only then can you start to believe. I appreciate that there is an element of luck on the way, however, as the golfer Gary Player once said, 'The harder you work the luckier you get'.

At 44 years of age, I have so many more deals waiting to happen, hundreds of new experiences to learn from and enjoy, and I genuinely wake up each day excited at what the day will bring. Many of the sales books I've read and continue to read come across like a textbook and remind me of being back at school. I wanted to write something for the educated salespeople, yet in a very light-hearted and humorous manner. Don't get me wrong, it's no Michael McIntyre autobiography, but there are plenty of stories that will make you laugh and are more memorable than a case study.

One of the great things about being in sales is that you never stop learning. The same applies to life, I guess. Every book I read, every training course I attend, I always take away at least three things that contribute to my performance in the wonderful game of sales.

I am not a writer, I am a performer, so I ask you to bear with me if my grammar isn't perfect. The syntax (I lifted that from another book, by the way) could be better and my punctuation could have been done by a four-year-old. I'm learning and the truth is that we all are, every day.

So with no further ado, please read on and enjoy. Kindly email me on tony@tonymorrisinternational.com to share your success.

About the Author

Tony Morris got married in 2006 to his beautiful wife, Shana, and now has two gorgeous children, Harry and Poppy.

Tony gained a 2:1 Honours degree in business and marketing from The University of Manchester, Manchester, United Kingdom, before travelling the world for a year. He has over 22 years' of experience in sales, both business to business and business to consumer, and has trained over 36,000 sales professionals in 43 industries. Tony started his career as a telesales consultant for the largest outsourced call centre, where he was involved in selling business to consumer (B2C) for one of the United Kingdom's biggest utility providers. He was awarded salesperson of the month for six consecutive months. He was then moved into a training role, where he wrote scripts and rebuttals, and trained every new consultant before they went on the phone.

Tony then moved into a business to business environment selling address management solutions. He started by cold-calling and generating appointments at director level and then sold in the field. He then progressed within a year, training a team of 14 telesales executives on how to make appointments from cold-calling and focusing his time on blue chip clients. In his four years at the company, he sold the highest value order of £725,000 over a three-year contract.

Alongside his business partner, Boyd Mayover, Tony's father-in-law, he set up a sales training company in May 2006 called Positive Approach. He started by cold-calling to generate appointments for both himself and his partner Boyd. Within the first year, they had 56 clients and this has continued to grow year on year. In six and a half years it has accumulated over 300 clients across 43 different industries.

In May 2019, Tony bought Boyd's shares in the business and Tony Morris International was born.

Tony's ethos is, 'You can sell any product or service with the right attitude and a well-planned call structure'.

Tony grew up in Borehamwood, Hertfordshire, and now lives in Radlett, Hertfordshire. He enjoys spending time with his wife, Shana, and his kids, Harry and Poppy, watching films, playing tennis and working out.

Many sales books that you will read will be written by many successful multimillionaires or people who claim to be ones. Tony is not one of those yet. He would love to sit here and say he has a different Ferrari for each day of the week, and he plays basketball on his helipad, but that simply would be a lie. He can say that 'he's working on it'. He earns a decent salary and has a very nice lifestyle. For once, he can see the light at the end of the tunnel and knows that it is possible to achieve what you set your heart on.

To Tony, the most satisfying realisation is that 'what you put in is what you get out' is now becoming a reality. It's taken him many years to see that, and there have been numerous bumps along the way. There will be many more to come, but he's grown to realise and understand that it's all part of the wonderful game of sales.

1
Introduction to Sales

'Success is the ability to move from one failure to another with no loss of enthusiasm'.

—Winston Churchill

I was born with what people call 'the gift of the gab'. I had to be the class clown and centre of attention, and my goal at school was to make people laugh. I knew I had a great day when I had everyone in stitches. I was over the moon when my parents returned from parents' evening and my dad had that expression plastered all over his face. My reports consistently said, 'He has lots of potential, but just doesn't use it. He's a very likeable and popular boy though and really makes people laugh all day long'. To me, that was the best report you could get; how naive I was! My parents' friends always used to say to me, 'You'll be a great salesman, as you've got an answer for everything and can talk the talk'.

My first boss in software sales taught me one of the most important lessons in sales that I have never forgotten – you have two ears and one mouth, use them accordingly. This is backed up by an Italian economist Vilfredo Pareto, who created a principle known as the Pareto's law – the 80/20 rule. It's a rule that can be applied to many scenarios, such as in retail, where they say 80% of your profit comes from 20% of your products. When applied to sales, if you are on the phone to a prospect, you should be speaking 20% and listening 80%. People love to talk, it's human nature, so let them. If people talk, they are comfortable; if they're comfortable, they like you; and if they like you, they are more likely to buy from you. Remember, we do *not* sell to anyone, we simply help them buy.

I had plenty of sales jobs growing up as a kid, from working in a call centre selling utilities, selling double glazing over the phone to selling newspaper subscriptions door to door. Looking back, I consider these roles part of my career in sales. It's from these positions that I was able to grow a real backbone and deal with the daily rejection that you learn is the nature of the beast as a salesman. It's not until you have heard these wonderful sentences of English –

'If you call me again I will come round to your house and kill your dog!'

'Can I have your home number?'

'No', I replied, 'I don't want people calling me at home'.

'Neither do I, so p*** off and go to hell!' –

that you start to learn not to take things too seriously to heart. It's all part of the fun game of sales and you need to become quicker and smarter to play the game to win.

This is not like any normal sales book you have read, or are likely to read again. I am telling you the way it is, not discussing the theory, which is like listening to your grandma's story for the 82nd time, about how she used to go to tea dances as a teenager.

I will give you real-life examples of both my and my clients' sales experiences, and the things that I have seen and learned over the last 16 years as a sales trainer. I will be discussing some of the best sales professionals I have had the good fortune to be in close contact, and the salespeople that you get apologising to you over the phone when you reply to their initial statement, 'It's not a good time'.

Many people often ask me, 'What are the key things you need to be a successful salesperson?' There are so many factors required to become super successful in selling, which I will explain in detail in this book, ranging from your tone, your questioning skills, your ability to listen, closing techniques and the list goes on.

Having interviewed many of the top 100 salespeople in the world (in my view) on my podcast, *Confessions of a Serial Seller*, I have been able to identify some traits amongst these legends. Coupled with analysing the top 1% of the 36,000 sales professionals I have been fortunate to work with, here are just a few of those traits explained in the following text.

Do Not Listen to Respond, Listen to Learn

Like I mentioned with Pareto's law, it should be 80% of them speaking and 20% of you listening. Most salespeople listen when it's their turn to speak. The most successful salespeople listen to learn. They take in everything that is being shared with them, because they understand that the prospect is far more important than they are. They understand that if they are speaking, they are not learning. They have seen that by allowing the prospect to speak and open up, not only do they share so much about themselves, but they provide information that will be beneficial to be used for proposing a solution.

In addition to this, as the prospect is speaking, they are often sharing things that were unplanned and on the surface not relevant to what you are there to discuss. However, when you are fully tuned in, you start to listen to what is not being shared, and I call this your opportunity antenna, which I will elaborate on in detail, later on in the book.

Asking Intelligent Questions

The vast majority of salespeople that I have been fortunate to work with ask really bad questions. And this is normally a bad habit that they have picked up over time. You are often unaware of the difficulties related with bad habits while doing them, as you are running on autopilot. It is not often that we sit back and reflect on what we are actually asking, to see if these questions can be improved.

Mindset

Every one of us has personal issues going on outside of work, some more serious than others. But if you bring these into work, it will have a negative impact on your performance and your personal problems will worsen, as you'll then create work problems as well. Some people like to look at a problem and moan about it. Others like to view it as a challenge and take pleasure coming up with a solution.

Which Person Are You?

There are some people who really like being negative, all the time, and they are cleverly called 'negative people'. You will always find negative people talking and moaning to other negative people, about how unfair everything is or how many problems there are at work. And you can guarantee they'll be moaning about the successful people and how easy they have things in their favour. As the saying goes, 'You become who you associate yourself with', so if you hang around with negative or lazy people all day long, your chances of achieving success decrease drastically, as they'll drain out all your positive energy. I call these people 'mood hoovers'. The great Jim Rohn said, 'You are the average of the five people you hang around with'; so, who do you hang around with on a regular basis? Are they serving you or draining you?

What I have found is A's will always hang around with other A's, whereas B's hang around with C's, to make them feel better about themselves.

I have a great friend who is very intelligent, very talented at what he does, yet at the age of 36 years, he has never progressed at work. It baffled me, as he seems driven, he's clearly good at what he does, he's well qualified and he wants to earn a good living, yet never seemed to make it. It was then clear to me that the friends he has grown up with all his life can be labelled as 'bums'. Some were unemployed and not looking for work, most of them took drugs, and none of them had any goals or real aspirations. Unfortunately, regularly hanging around with them clearly held him back, as it's all he sees and knows. Don't get me wrong, to break away from your lifelong friends is not an easy task, but is leaving a partner who physically abuses you an easy task? It depends what you want out of life and what your priorities are.

Thomas Edison, the inventor of the light bulb, was interviewed many years ago. The interviewer said to him, 'You have tried to make this light bulb ten thousand times and failed, how can you possibly carry on?' Edison laughed at the interviewer and said, 'You are both naive and ignorant, I have learned ten thousand ways of how it should not be done'. A fine example of how any situation can be viewed very differently.

I heard a story where a relatively new shoe manufacturer brought out some trainers that were unique in the market. The company tried to penetrate the UK market and failed miserably. It sent two of their sales teams to Africa, to test the market's appetite. After a few days, the first salesperson called the boss and said, 'This is the biggest waste of time ever, I may as well come home immediately'. The boss was really surprised to hear that and asked, 'What makes you say that?' The salesperson replied, 'because no one here wears any shoes'.

A couple of days later, the boss asked the second salesperson while answering his call, 'Tell me, how are you finding things?' The excited salesperson says, 'It's incredible, you are going to have to send me out a lot more samples'. The boss was totally taken aback by this response. He says, 'Really, how come?' The salesperson says, 'It's amazing, no one here wears any shoes'.

Which Salesperson Would You Have Been?

One of the wonderful things about sales is that there's no such thing as failure, it's all feedback. We can all learn from our successes as well as our failures. The great Nelson Mandela once said, 'You never lose, either you win or you learn'.

The Lesson

When the top sales performers make a prospecting call, they always look for a lesson. So, if they reach a gatekeeper and are unable to be put through to the decision-maker, rather than returning frustrated, they ask themselves, 'What is the lesson?' What could I have said differently on that call to have received a different outcome? They will reflect on the questions they asked, the statements they made and consider where things went off the track.

Is that how you view things, when things don't go your way on a call?

The Whale

The other thing the top sales performers do, when making a prospecting call, is to picture the prospect in their mind. They consider the key decision-makers as their potential VIP clients. I have labelled these people as 'the whales'. Let me explain what I mean.

In my business, I usually land up two whales a year – a total of 34 whales till date. No matter what marketing I undertake, the number of prospecting calls I make, I always land up two whales a year. A whale to me is a client that has invested £75,000 on training or speaking engagements. Every single call I make, in my mind, the person I am speaking with is the whale. This changes my perspective on a call. As I consider the person at the other end of the phone to be the whale, it changes my focus. My concentration is heightened, my listening is finely tuned and I am laser focused on that call, and every distraction around me is blocked out.

I recall that in September 2015, I boarded the train to meet Ian Maclean, the franchise director of Belvoir. They are an estate and letting agency franchisee with over 150 offices. We were meeting to discuss me delivering sales training to their entire network. It was probably the largest opportunity for my business, and I spent hours preparing for the meeting. I carried out mystery calls to many of the franchisees, posing as a landlord and as a buyer, as I wanted to see how the franchisees handled my enquiry. I listened back to calls, so I could write detailed feedback, as I wanted to provide Ian with as much value as possible.

I met Ian at their Mornington Crescent office and waited nervously in the reception. I knew you should treat every meeting exactly the same, but I was aware of how big an opportunity this could be, it was difficult to stay calm and composed.

I met a lady, who kindly offered me tea and walked me to Ian's office. Ian stood and shook my hand and had a really welcoming smile, which immediately put my nerves at ease.

We sat and started chatting about how he got into the property market and his experience working with Belvoir. I explained to him about the different estate and letting agents I had trained and most importantly the results I'd help them achieve. I told Ian I carried out mystery calls and asked if he'd like to hear my feedback and findings. He was so impressed that I'd gone to all that effort and was really keen to hear my findings. I shared feedback on the three calls I had carried out and highlighted all the different areas that I would have developed, had I been training them. Ian agreed with everything I had said, and felt I had raised some really great points.

And then he said, 'Tony, you seem like a great guy and clearly know your stuff, "but". . .'.

And as soon as I heard the 'but', I was devastated. I tried to not show the disappointment on my face, but it was a struggle. I got my hopes up so much for this meeting, and they were gone in a flash.

Ian went on to say that they have an in-house training department, and he just felt I didn't offer anything different enough to what they do. I really didn't know how to handle that objection, especially as all my excitement had evaporated in a matter of seconds.

I left his office flat. The exact opposite to how I felt going in. I know that in sales you don't win them all, but I really thought this was my time and this was going to be the big one. On the train journey back, I was going through the entire conversation and trying to work out what I could have said differently, to have received a different outcome.

I sent Ian a follow-up email the following day, thanking him for his time.

Even though I was so disappointed, my late dad always told me that you never know when a person might turn up in your life again, so no matter what happens, don't burn bridges, and don't show your disappointment.

About eight months later, I got an email from Ian, introducing me to a guy called Eric Walker. Ian explained that Eric was his equivalent, for another estate agency franchise called Northwood. He said, they're not as big as Belvoir, have about 80 offices and they're considering

training for their franchisees, and he wanted to introduce me. I thanked him and organised a meeting with
Eric at a lovely restaurant at London King's Cross.

I thought about my late dad and his advice and felt
this was a sign. I didn't want to get my hopes up, like I
did with Ian, but I was excited to meet Eric.

I turned up at the restaurant to meet Eric, and he was
sitting there with another gentleman. Eric introduced
him and then introduced me to his colleague Phil Gee.
Eric explained that he looks after the 50 franchisees in
the north and Phil looks after 40 of them in the south.
Phil is also considering the same type of sales training he
wants for his network.

We sat down and got the niceties out the way; where
we have all travelled from, where we live, etc. And then
we ordered some lunch. Eric asked, 'red or white?' and
I said, 'I like both, so whichever you prefer', and he
ordered a bottle of merlot. As we were waiting for the
wine, we started talking business. Phil started talking
about the challenges he sees across his 40 franchisees,
and they were mainly a lack of properties to sell or let
and the franchisees struggling to charge higher fees than
their competitors. I was listening very attentively and
was taking notes as he talked. Eric was nodding in agreement with everything Phil was sharing. Once Phil had
stopped talking, I said to Eric, 'Are you seeing the same
things in your network of franchisees?' He said,
'Absolutely. It's a common challenge we see and no matter how much training they get on it, they just can't seem
to implement it into their daily routine'. I said, 'So what

training have they had, to try and help them win more property and command higher fees?' Eric replied, 'Loads, we have an internal training department, and all franchisees spend their first four weeks in training, when they join Northwood. And then there is a whole training calendar running throughout the year, and they can select which course they want for themselves or their team and then attend'.

Eric then said, 'Ian spoke very highly of you, and I can see why, "but"....'.

There goes that bloody 'but' again!

And he continued to say, 'Our franchisees just won't pay those sorts of fees, especially as they can get it internally. I'm not doubting your training and it will be better than what we do internally, but I just know how our franchisees think'.

Our wine was poured and lunch was served. They were both lovely, but it would have tasted a lot nicer had I not heard that damn 'but' for the second time. The three of us just talked about life and property and enjoyed our lunch. I felt compelled to pay for the bill, thinking they would never accept and how wrong I was. So, not only had I lost the deal, it cost me £260 in the process.

I wasn't as disappointed as I was on the train back from meeting Ian, as I didn't get my hopes up as much. I guess that was one positive I took from the experience.

A few months passed and I got an email from Eric, asking if I was available on the 15th July 2016?

I replied, 'Yes, why do you ask?'

He went on to say that Northwood was having its annual conference and he'd like me to be their headline speaker. And he asked if we can set up a call to discuss the brief. It took me all of 12 seconds to reply with dates on which I was available to speak; it would have been 3 seconds, but I didn't want to appear too keen.

We spoke a few days later, discussed the brief, discussed my fees and he booked me.

I delivered my talk at Northwood and sat back down at my table at the front. A gentleman on my right leaned in and said, 'That was fantastic', and he passed me his business card and asked me to call him next week. He was Duncan, the MD of a company called Jelf, which I'd never heard of. I didn't want to ask what they did, as I didn't want to embarrass myself.

Later on in the conference, I was getting myself a cup of tea and a gentleman approached me and said, 'I loved your talk, really inspiring'. I said, 'Thank you so much, really nice of you to say that. What do you do?'

He said, 'My name is Dorian, and I am the CEO of Belvoir'. He explained that they are going to conduct a conference in a few months and if I am available, he'd like me to speak. I said, 'Yes, I'd love to', and we swapped business cards.

A couple of weeks later, Dorian's PA emailed me and organised a call for Dorian and me. We spoke, I confirmed my availability and my fees and I was booked.

Three months later, I was standing on stage at Belvoir's property conference in front of over 400 people. I was the last speaker of the day. I delivered my talk, and then Dorian took the stage to round up the conference and welcome everyone to the bar. I followed the crowd and made my way to the bar.

I got a drink and was chatting to a couple of the delegates. During the conversation, a guy approached me and said, 'I'm sorry to interrupt you, but have you got a couple of minutes?' I had no idea who he was or what he wanted, but I said, 'Sure'.

We went over to his table, and he introduced himself as David and explained he was the MD of Newton Fallowell. He said, 'We're an estate agency franchise, not as big as Belvoir, but we have 45 franchisees. We would love to have you speak at our conference in four months' time'. I was delighted and said, 'Of course, that would be great'. He gave me his card and told me to call his PA on Monday and set up a call. I went back to the table where I was talking to a couple of delegates and continued our chat.

A week later, I was booked to speak at Newton Fallowell's conference.

The conference was certainly the smallest of the three; however, as always, I gave it my all. David had kindly invited me to stay for the black tie gala that evening, so I could meet all the franchisees. At my table I was sitting next to a lady called Michelle and her colleague Liz. Michelle told me she ran a mortgage company called Brook FS and Liz was her right-hand woman. They were great company, and we had a lovely evening. After dinner, we were drinking at the bar and Michelle asked me about my training company and what courses I deliver. She gave me her number and asked for a call on Monday, as she felt her sales team needed a boost.

We caught up on Monday as promised, had a great chat and she booked me to deliver a three-day training to her team. On the first evening of training, I was having a drink with the team and Liz. Liz asked me if I had ever done any work with recruitment companies, to which I explained I had and how I helped them. She said that she mentioned me to her husband Steve and what I was doing with her team, and he wanted to meet me.

Steve and I met in London about three weeks later, and he brought his MD Adam along, from Sterling Recruitment. They explained in detail about their business and that they're having their first ever conference and would like me to be their speaker. We agreed to it at once.

I spoke at their conference, and Adam said they needed me in the business, as their consultants could really do with my help. A month later, I was delivering training to all his team.

The following week, I was delivering training to Duncan's team at Jelf, who was sitting next to me at the Northwood conference. This was part of a six-month training program, as they had over 80 people to train. The team was getting such incredible results because of the training that they asked me to work with their sister company SME. They had several teams and booked me to deliver a training of around 12 days. On one of those training days, I was introduced to a guy called Paul, who was the MD for a company called Bluefin. He asked if I deliver sales management training, and I explained my company does, but not me. I set him up for a meeting with my sales management expert John Bullock, and they ended up booking him for a nine-day leadership program.

Everyone at SME was talking about the increase in their average order values and they couldn't believe how quickly my techniques worked.

A couple of weeks passed, and I got a call from a guy called Lee. He explained that we never got to meet, but he was one of the directors at SME and left quite recently and was now the MD of Premier Business Care. He asked me to come and meet him at his offices, as he wanted to see if I felt I could help his team. It took a few weeks to organise and as they had five teams of 25 people to train, they booked me for a four-month program.

I was doing some training in Watford, with one of Belvoir's franchisees, and Ian Maclean happened to be spending the morning there. As soon as I saw him, it hit me like a tonne of bricks. Ian was my whale, I just didn't realise it at the time. On the back of meeting him, my company generated over £800,000 of business.

What's interesting to me is, out of the 34 whales I have landed up to date, 28 were tadpoles who happened to know the whale. Remember, everyone you know, knows someone you don't. I started to understand that the decision-maker on the other side of the call might not be the whale; however, they might know the whale. Again, this was a wake-up call, to ensure I do my very best on every single call I make or take in my business.

To help remind me of this concept, I have surrounded my home office with whales. My daughter Poppy is aware of this concept, and she is always on the lookout for whales wherever we go. I bought her a bracelet with a whale's fin and she makes me whales out of the materials she buys, as she adores arts and crafts. Figure 1.1 shows my most recent whale she bought me, which sits below my monitor, as a daily reminder that your next sales call could be your whale, or could know a whale. This visual reminder has helped me build the habit, and reprogram my brain to think differently.

Figure 1.1

The secret I have started to understand is sales comes down to two factors:

Be boringly consistent, and do the basics, brilliantly.

I know these two things do not sound very inspiring and, if anything, a little deflating; however, these two things are the exact opposite of what salespeople do.

The vast majority of salespeople I have had the pleasure to train are consistently inconsistent. And they invest 80% of their time doing the 20% of things that need to be done.

Tenacity

Another trait that I have seen through the most successful salespeople is how tenacious they are. One rule that has stood me in good stead throughout my career is to never give up until the prospect gives me a damn good reason as to why they feel my product or service is not right for them or their business. Only once I feel that is a fair justification will I then keep going, just changing my angle to create new opportunities.

There is only one caveat to this, are they a prospect or a suspect? It means there will be some companies that are just not the right fit for your products or services and that's okay. You cannot work with everyone and you wouldn't want too. They are who I label as suspects, you just move straight on and invest as little time with them as possible. Later in the book, I will be talking about grading your clients and truly understanding your target audience. One you have niched down and are crystal clear on who you serve, it becomes much easier to find them.

Many people often say, 'Sales is a numbers game', which could not be further from the truth. I am one of the worst footballers you could ever meet, and if I took 100 penalties against an average keeper, I may score three only by pure luck. Consider a footballer with some ability, who practised on a regular basis, developed their penalty-taking skills and then shot hundred penalties against an average keeper, do you think they might score more than three goals? So it's a probability game, meaning the better you are and the more you do, the higher the probability of achieving your desired outcomes.

This ties nicely into a trait of super successful sellers. They are more productive than their peers. They will number-crunch much more often than anyone in their sales. And although they make plenty of mistakes along the way, they are also learning from them. And because they are having many more sales conversations, they are getting in much more practice than others, which builds their confidence and skills.

Once I started to understand this, my mindset started to shift. I often think back to a time when I was travelling in Sydney, Australia. I was eight months into my travels and had almost run out of money. I had to get my head around the frightening reality of having to return home, return to a normal life and find a job. I was chatting to an Aussie guy on Bondi Beach who looked the spitting image of Mick Jagger in his younger years. I was moaning about my financial situation when he said, 'I have been running a direct sales operation for the past six years selling encyclopaedias, and I have 130 sales reps selling door to door. Why don't you come and work for me?'

Intrigued, I asked him, 'How does it work?', and he took me back to his house, which I can only describe as the most beautiful castle I had ever laid eyes on. In his office, he showed me a giant map of Sydney and the surrounding areas all highlighted in different colours, which marked the different sales reps' territories. He showed me what would be my territory, handed me a 2800-page book and a rucksack, and said, 'You need to go knocking doors and have to close on the day. Every encyclopaedia you sell will earn you $150, cash in hand'. I was out of the door before he said 'hand', and on I went.

I started the following morning and left my hostel at 08:30 a.m. to walk to my first road in 79°F heat. I was so keen and had already spent my new earned commission in my head. I arrived at the start of my first road and excitedly knocked on my first door. After eight knocks, I realised this was what they describe in sales as time-wasting. I knocked on my second, then my third, my fourth door, and by my fifth door with no answer, I started to wonder whether these houses were actually inhabited.

It wasn't until my eighth door where a cute older lady aged around 107 answered the knock. She had to fetch her hearing aid to hear my pitch. *Great start,*

I thought to myself, *the first person I actually get to pitch to is deaf.*

After 25 minutes of screaming at her and watching patiently as she fiddled with her hearing aid, I made the executive decision that I was barking up the wrong tree and I went on. I kept on knocking, and on my 34th door, a young guy opened the door and I saw my opportunity.

As soon as I uttered the words 'Hi, my name is Tony', the door slammed shut in my face. I started having second thoughts and looked at my watch to realise I'd been walking a total of 33 minutes and I was already considering quitting. I remembered my dad's words, 'In sales, you never quit', and I went on.

I must have knocked on about 75 doors and spoken to one person who allowed me to get my pitch out, to which he replied quite politely, 'Never come here again'. When I realised he was the nicest person I'd spoken to all day, I realised I chose the wrong area and came back to the hostel.

The following day my alarm rang at 07:55 a.m. and I jumped in the shower and got out on the road, full of the same level of enthusiasm as yesterday morning. I chanted to myself, 'New day, new opportunities'.

By 16:45 p.m., the 12 people I spoke to had all told me where to go, and my chant at home was very different.

When I woke up the following day, I was going to give it my final go, as maybe sales just wasn't for me. I went on my way and got an answer at my first door. The lady let me get my two minute pitch out, to which she replied, 'How much?', in a shocked intake of breath. I explained that the encyclopaedias are normally retailed at $499; however, we were running an amazing promotion and selling them for only $399 (word by word what my script said), and she invited me in.

I almost high-fived her, but thought that may show a sign of desperation, so I only mentally high-fived. She kindly made me a cold drink and started to look through the huge book that I had been carrying on my back for the past 48 hours.

Her husband came down the stairs to join us, and within a matter of seconds, kindly asked me to leave. I left to him shouting at her to not invite strangers in.

I went straight back to Mr Jagger's castle to return his stupid, unsellable books. With sweat on my brow and big sweat rings under my arms, he looked at me like some vagrant and said, 'You look a mess, let me get you a drink'. My second invitation in three days, although I was pretty confident he wouldn't listen to my pitch either.

I said, 'I simply don't believe anyone sells these things'. He laughed and said, 'I have one question for you, how many doors did you knock on a day?' Surprised by his question, I shrugged my shoulders and said, 'I didn't really count, but I guess around 70 a day'.

He replied, 'I chose not to share this with you, as I wanted you to learn for yourself; however, all my reps measure their figures. They have proven that you must knock on a minimum of 100 doors per day. Only nine people will listen to your pitch, and six of them will tell you where to go, some politely and some not. Three, however, will invite you in. Two of these will politely tell you a reason why they can't buy today such as "I need to think about it", "I don't have the money", "I'm not sure I'll use it", etc. However, one will buy; guaranteed. The numbers never lie'. To say I was sceptical was an understatement, and I remember saying, 'I knocked on at least 200 doors throughout the three days'.

He interrupted me and reiterated, '100 per day minimum'. He said, 'You have two days left in this week. Surely, it's worth trying. Or maybe sales are not your bag, and you should look for a different path'.

With that, I grabbed my book back and went on my way. Fourteen, no answer. Fifteen, no answer. Sixteen, the door opened. 'Hi, my name is Tony Morris and I have an incredible promotion, available for today only'. He listened to my pitch and then slammed the door in my face. Before screaming obscenities through his letter box, I took a deep breath and thought about what Mr Jagger had said.

'Nine will listen, and six will tell you where to go'.

So, I had eight to go, according to him. I kept on knocking and number 31 invited me in. She sat me down and listened intently, then dropped the bombshell. 'I need to think about it'. On the outside I was smiling, although I was pretty sure she could see me grinding my teeth in anger. But, keeping the tally, I continued my walk.

Lucky number 67 was Mr Peterson, and to this day I remember that feeling as he pulled out his cheque book.

I called Mr Jagger to arrange an encyclopaedia to be delivered to the door and restrained myself from screaming down the phone. I calmly switched my mobile off and continued grinning.

As he shook my hand, I went in for the man hug, to which he stood there still as a mannequin as I hugged him, until I realised I was invading his personal space. I skipped out of his house and did one of those jumps where you click your heels together, and I almost tripped over his front garden.

I carried on knocking, as I was convinced to be on a lucky streak. Thirty-three rejections later, I went back to the hostel with the biggest smile on my face and a feeling I will never forget.

I continued this job for the next six weeks and my feelings towards having the door slammed in my face took a full 360° turn. When door number 24 was slammed hard in my face, I clenched a fist of delight and muttered to myself, 'Only 66 to go until I get somewhere'.

Mr Jagger was right, the figures never lied. People thought I was actually insane when they shouted at me, 'I never want to see your face again!', and I replied with a big grin plastered across my face. 'Good, you are the 59th person to say that to me today, so I need 31 more of them!'

This was one of my first, yet most vital, lessons in sales, it's a probability game. As long as you learn your pitch well, and give it the same level of enthusiasm and passion every opportunity you get, you cannot fail.

Why Do People Buy?

To be super successful in sales, it is imperative that we understand why someone buys.

Psychologists have said that there are two reasons why anyone buys anything – pain and gain. Therefore, people are looking to either avoid pain or gain pleasure. If you think of every single purchase you have ever made, it will come down to those two things.

If you are absolutely starving, you grab a burger at McDonalds, to avoid the hunger pain. If it is your wedding anniversary, you take your partner somewhere very special, this is to gain pleasure. You could argue that it's also to avoid the pain they'd give you if you don't take them somewhere nice, or, worse, forget it's the anniversary.

You pay taxes to avoid going to prison, and you book a holiday to gain pleasure. You get the idea.

Psychologists have also stated that avoiding pain is two and a half times more of a driving factor than gaining pleasure. Therefore, the majority of your sales conversations should be focused on the problems you solve, the issues you minimise and the challenges you eradicate.

I have never seen myself as a salesperson; I see myself as a problem solver. Our job is not to sell; it's to help people buy.

Why?

Because nobody likes to be sold too. Think of the last time someone tried to sell to you. You walk into a furniture store and a salesperson jumps on you, 'How can I help?' This is before my second foot has landed on the shop floor; I call this commission breath.

If you have watched the film *Glengarry Glen Ross*, one of my favourite old sales classics films, which is where I got the name, 'Coffee's for closers', you would have heard in Alec Baldwin's famous monologue, 'ABC – Always Be Closing'. And the point he makes is accurate, just the way he portrays it is a little out of date. Please do not get me wrong; you need to 'ask' for the order to close the business, but in today's world of sales, there are different ways to close the sale, without coming across as a direct, aggressive and arrogant salesperson. The elements that Alec Baldwin alluded to are still appropriate and relevant today – be tenacious, don't take no for an answer. However, he also makes the valid points that if they walk on the car plot, they want to buy, so sell them a car. In an inbound world, this might be fair; in an outbound world, you have called them, so a different type of sales approach is needed altogether.

In today's world, I believe ABC is 'Always Be Curious'. The truth is, people love to talk about themselves, so let them. And if they're talking about themselves, they're comfortable; if they're comfortable, they'll be warm to you; and if they are warm to you, they are more likely to want to buy from you.

Therefore, the quicker you understand that your job is to solve a prospect's problems, as opposed to sell them your product or service, the more sales you'll start to make.

The great Zig Ziglar once said, 'If you can help enough people get what they want, you can get everything in life you want'. And I took so much value from that saying. If we can genuinely look to service, to help and to solve, then we are more likely to get what we are looking to achieve. I was lucky enough to have Zig Ziglar's son, Tom Ziglar, on my podcast, *Confessions of a Serial Seller*, as he now looks after his father's legacy, the Ziglar Corporation. And I loved one anecdote he shared with me. The day he was born, Zig put a post in the newspaper that read, 'Today, a salesman has been born'.

This way of thinking is validated in some of the greatest sales books ever written. One of my favourites is *The Go-Giver* by Bob Burg. His entire ethos is based on this simple yet super powerful premise – if you give first, you will gain second. I have practised this concept for many years, and its incredible how powerful and effective it really is. And you feel good doing it. In a later chapter, I will expand on this game-changing concept.

2
It Is Not Just About the Destination

'All our dreams can come true, if we have the courage to pursue them'.

—Walt Disney

As an ambitious entrepreneur, I am constantly striving to push my team to achieve new heights. The problem with this is you don't give yourself a pat on the back during the journey. With the help of my coach, Graeme Godfrey, I've learned to reward the journey, not just the destination.

My wife Shana sent me this post on 9 November 2012 (Figure 2.1).

Figure 2.1

This was the day my first self-published book *Coffee's for Closers* arrived at our house. It was a special moment for us.

Ten years later, on that same day, I was flying from London (Heathrow) to Atlanta, Georgia (Figure 2.2).

Figure 2.2

The reason for flying to Atlanta was to record 336 videos at Jeb Blount's studio. These videos will be going on his incredible platform, Sales Gravy, to share with his huge, and well deserved, sales tribe.

If you haven't heard of Jeb Blount, then you clearly haven't read many sales books. Apart from writing 15 bestselling books, all published by Wiley, he is a sales guru. I have read every single one of his books and studied this man for the last 12 years.

If you ask anyone with interest in football who are the three best footballers in the world, alive or dead, depending on which country they're from, you're most likely to hear, Pele, Messi and Ronaldo.

If you ask most salespeople – who take their profession seriously, which you are one by the way, otherwise you wouldn't be reading this – who are the three best salespeople in the world, alive or dead, depending on which country they're from, you're most likely to hear, Zig Ziglar, Jim Rohn and Tony Morris. I'm kidding about the third one; they'd say, Jeb Blount.

The following picture (Figure 2.3) is the new front cover of the revised edition of *Coffee's for Closers*, which, in case you didn't realise, is what you're reading right now.

TONY MORRIS

Coffee's for

CLOSERS

THE BEST
REAL LIFE
SALES BOOK
YOU'LL EVER
READ

WILEY

Figure 2.3

I share this story because if you'd have said to me, in November 2012, 10 years from the day my first book *Coffee's for Closers* arrived at my house, that I'd be on a plane to Atlanta to record sales videos in Jeb Blount's studio, and there was a second edition of my book, which was published by Wiley, I would have asked which narcotics you'd have taken and called a paramedic.

But that is exactly what happened. And I don't share this to show off, I share this to demonstrate my point. It's not just about the destination, it's also about the journey.

If you choose to take your sales profession seriously, then you will have the most incredible journey ahead of you. Notice that I said, 'if you choose', because it is a choice. It's 'your choice' and most people take the choice to 'not' take it that seriously. They see it as a nine-to-five job, and that's okay, I'm not here to judge.

But if you make that choice, you commit to it and you graft as hard as you possibly can, then your journey will be a special one.

You will experience 'limiting beliefs'. Everyone does and I still have some. I first saw Anthony Robbins speak in November 2011 in London. During this three-day conference, I first learned about limiting beliefs. Robbins explained that the most damaging voice we listen to is our own. We tell ourselves all the reasons why we can't achieve something and why it's not even worth attempting it.

Had Roger Bannister taken notice of his limiting belief in 1954, he would not have been the first man in history to conquer the four-minute mile. Once Bannister proved it was possible, about 10 people beat his record in the following eight months.

As I was listening to Robbins's powerful and hypnotic voice, I started to hear my limiting beliefs echo in my head, 'I got a C in GCSE English, I couldn't write a book'. 'Even if I wrote a book, who in their right mind is going to read it'. At that time, I had written 20 pages of *Coffee's for Closers*. I had stopped at page 21, because my inner critic told me I wasn't good enough. In his book, *The Chimp Paradox*, Dr Steve Peters explains this concept in much greater depth.

It wasn't until I 'chose' to take onboard Tony Robbins's advice did I continue to write. It took me a further 12 months to complete it, and in its first month of release, it became the Amazon #1 bestseller.

And 10 years later, you're reading the second edition.

Could you imagine the life you could lead, if you were able to ignore that inner voice? If 'you chose' to ignore the limiting belief and do it anyway.

I have so many more goals to hit, including delivering a keynote at a sales kick-off conference on stage in Vegas, in front of 10,000 salespeople. And although this gig has not yet happened, I am very confident it will. The Tony watching Anthony Robbins in London Excel in November 2011 would not have even dreamed about speaking on stage in Vegas, in front of 10,000 salespeople, as that Tony didn't think that big. But the current Tony not only thinks it, he actually believes it too.

Set a goal.

Graft like mad.

And watch your dreams come true.

3
Give, and You Shall Gain

'The secret of getting ahead is getting started'.

—Mark Twain

I mentioned at the beginning of this book about a fantastic book called *The Go-Giver* by Bob Burg and John Mann. As you read the following stories, I sincerely hope that you too can see the value in this genius concept.

I was having a face-to-face meeting with Paul from Exane BNP Paribas, a large Parisian bank that you may be familiar with. We were discussing the possibility of me speaking at a sales event they were running in London. They wanted me as the final speaker, so as to end the event with a bang. I asked all the discovery questions as you'd expect – what is your ideal outcome from the event? What is the biggest problem you would like your sales team to overcome? Let's fast forward one month after the event, how do you know it has been successful?

He answered them all and we had a great chat. I asked, 'What are your plans for the evening after the event?' He said, 'I am looking to have some sort of team-building activity. We don't get together enough, especially after going through the pandemic. So, I am thinking of go-karting or an escape room, not yet decided. We shook hands, I told him I'd get a proposal over to him and I left.

I headed to my next meeting in Reading, to meet Virgin Experience, one of the many brands of Richard Branson's empire. I had been recommended to this company, and was meeting the MD whom I wasn't recommended to. We had a good 30-minute meeting and we both got talking about sales books and self-development books. I mentioned one of my personal favourites, *S.U.M.O. (Shut Up, Move On)* by Paul McGee, and she'd never heard of it. We talked about the different experiences Virgin did and I asked which was her most popular, and she replied, 'Escape rooms by far'. It was as if a light bulb blew in my head. I said, 'Would you mind if I make a call right now?' She hesitantly said, 'Okay, if you need too'. I called Paul from Exane BNP and said, 'Paul, just a quick one, have you booked your escape room yet?' He replied, 'No, not yet'. I said, 'I'm going to introduce you to Virgin Experiences, they are a team-building company and their escape rooms are by far their most popular experience'. I'll CC you into an email with their MD. He said, 'Thanks Tony, and thanks so much for thinking of us'. I put the phone down and said,

'I think I got you a lead'. She smiled, and said, 'It did sound like it'.

We continued our chat, and she thanked me for coming in and asked for a proposal, as they were speaking to a couple of other sales training companies as well. We agreed to a follow-up call and I left. I got in my car, went straight to Amazon and ordered a copy of *S.U.M.O* to be sent to her office. I am not saying I won both Exane BNP and Virgin Experiences, because of both those things, but it didn't hurt.

What I learned from *The Go-Giver* concept of Bob Burg and John Mann is that people like to repay you once you have helped them.

In Dr Robert Cialdini's book, *Influence: Science and Practice*, he referred to this concept as 'the law of reciprocity'.

Therefore, if we can give first, we are most likely to get back. There are two points worth considering here. Firstly, you won't always be able to give. Secondly, when you are able to give, you will not always get back.

On that note, there is one amazing tip I was once given by one of my speaking mentors, Casper Berry, amongst the greatest speakers ever on risk taking. He taught me the 'givers gain' concept.

Casper said, 'One of the best ways to get into a speaking bureau is to offer them an opportunity first and then they are likely to take you on as a speaker in their bureau'. Again, so simple, yet genius.

About three weeks later, I got an enquiry from an MD to book me for a property conference. We discussed the brief, my availability and fees and he booked me. He then asked me, 'You don't happen to know any economist speakers, do you?' I said, 'I don't, but I know someone who will'. I then took Casper's advice and called a bureau called 'Champions', which I was keen to work with. I gave them the speaking opportunity and they found an economist speaker for them. Not only am I now on Champions' books, but I have already been booked by them.

I got an enquiry in October 2022 from a company called Baker Ing International Limited. They are a debt collection company, founded by Lisa Baker-Reynolds. She emailed me, asking to arrange a call to discuss training her sales team. On our first call, I asked the same question I ask every enquirer, 'Who recommended you to me?' I ask this question for two reasons. One, it gets you the source of the enquiry. This helps you understand which part of your marketing works and then you can invest more money in that area. Second, it gives the perception that your business comes from recommendations, which is a great seed to plant so early on. Remember, perception is reality; if they think it is, then it is. Lisa replied, 'You trained me nine years ago at Creditsafe, and I have been following you ever since'. This demonstrated to me that you never know when someone in your past could turn up in your future, which is why you should never burn bridges, as you just don't know when you will need that person later down the line.

Lisa and I had a great chat, I qualified the opportunity and then arranged to send a proposal and the next call.

During that conversation we talked about rugby, and Lisa shared that she took her clients to the England vs. Wales game and was looking to invite clients to a box for the England vs. South Africa game in November. I asked if she'd organised the tickets and she explained she hadn't. I told her that one of my oldest clients is Corinthian Sports, the leading corporate hospitality company in the UK. I have trained Corinthian's sales team for the last 12 years; however, I had not worked with them for about the past 18 months due to the pandemic. I promised Lisa I'd make an introduction to the MD, Gavin. The introduction was sent and within a week Lisa had booked a box for the England vs. South Africa game. Gavin called to thank me and kindly gave me two tickets to the game. He said, 'Invite anyone you want, it's going to be the most fantastic atmosphere'. He followed by saying, 'Can you come to our London offices? We are expanding rapidly and might need your help', and we organised a meeting.

I got off the phone to Gavin and knew immediately who I was going to call, my old client, Eric, who was MD of Northwood, the property franchise company. Eric was now the MD of Martin & Co, another property franchise, which is part of The Property Franchise Group (TPFG) consisting of nine brands of franchises and more than 600 branches across the UK. As a pure coincidence, I have been dealing with Gareth, the CEO of the TPFG. I called Eric to ask if he was available, and he was ecstatic. We booked it in the diary and organised which pub we'd be meeting at, before the game.

Corinthian went on to book me for a £49,000 project, to help build a new sales team in their new offices.

Gareth at TPFG called me and said, 'Eric has just called me and gave you the most shining review, of the work you did whilst he was at Northwood'. Gareth then booked me to run a series of webinars to promote across their nine brands.

A few days later, I then saw a post on LI from one of the sales team at Baker Ing International, asking if anyone knows a publisher for her mum's book. I put her in touch with my publisher Wiley. Again, I don't know if that's why I won Baker Ing as a client, but it did not hurt.

Now I am not saying I landed all the three opportunities because I gave first, but it did not hurt. This reinforced to me the power of 'givers gain' and it is something I continue to do, wherever possible.

4
Every Second Counts

'I've missed more than 9000 shots. I've lost almost 300 games. For 26 times I've been trusted to take the game-winning shot and missed. I've failed over and over and over again in my life, and that is why I succeed'.

—Michael Jordon

In sales, time is your most powerful weapon. Equally, it is your most powerful enemy. If used effectively, it can propel you to another level of success. If used incorrectly, it can drain you and be your biggest obstacle.

One great way to use time effectively is creating templates. I have developed templates for every single scenario that I have come across and wanted to share them with you.

So, imagine you had a great meeting, agreed to send a proposal and organised the second call. You then send the proposal as promised, and the prospect does not take the second call. However, they do email you apologising for missing your call and say they will call you in the next day or so and then don't call. You then make another attempt and leave a voice mail, which they don't respond to. You leave it a few days and then call again and do not leave a voice mail. You then send them this email:

Subject line: NAME, is this still something you want to do?

Dear NAME,

When we last spoke you said. . . . . (highlight all the positives of what they said in bullet points).

Clearly, things have changed, as I have not been able to get hold of you since. If you have decided to not go ahead, that's fine, I won't take any offence. All I ask you to provide is your real feedback as to why you felt this wasn't for you.

I am always looking to develop as a person and any feedback on me or our service is invaluable, so please kindly come back to me.

I sincerely look forward to hearing from you.

Kindest regards,

Tony

If the prospect has ignored you for around four to five weeks, and you have made five or six attempts to reach them, then I recommend the email provided in the following text. It's using reverse psychology and shows the prospect that you do not need their work, which is a much more appealing position than to come across as desperate:

Subject line: NAME, I'll take it as a no

Hi NAME,

I hope you're well.

I have not heard back from you after sharing the proposal. I am going to take it as a no, as I don't want you to feel embarrassed to have to come back to me and tell me that. When this becomes a more pressing priority, please come back to me, and if I am not fully booked, we can discuss it.

Thanks,

Tony

You know when you have been dealing with a prospect and everything seems to be progressing nicely, and then they suddenly stop taking your calls? They stop replying to your emails, and you can never get hold of them.

They call this, 'being ghosted'. The email template that I have found the most effective way to get them to reply is provided in the following text, and this is the final resort. If you don't get a reply from this, then it's time to move on:

Subject line: NAME, Have I offended you?

Hey NAME,

I hope you are well. I am concerned if I have done something that has offended or upset you. The last time I spoke to you on 14 June, you kindly explained you have a few new starters and wanted to arrange a one-day induction training with them all, in the end of July, and asked me to call you to organise. Since then, I have left numerous messages and sent many emails and have not heard back from you.

I know you are busy; however, after working together successfully for nearly a year, I was hoping for some response and I am just concerned if I have done something that's bothered you.

Please come back to me to let me know, and I hope to hear from you soon.

Kindest regards,

Tony

I use the following email for responding to an enquiry that I have been unable to get hold of:

Dear NAME,

Thank you for enquiring about. . . . . . .

As a senior consultant at X company, I have over X years' success in helping companies like you achieve a, b and c. I am keen to talk to you and discuss how I can help your company as well.

I have tried calling you on numerous occasions this week with no success, so if you can kindly let me know when is a convenient time to speak and we can discuss your specific requirements and how I can help.

I look forward to hearing from you.

Kindest regards,

Tony

The following email is used post-meeting, to outline a summary and the clearly defined next steps:

Dear NAME,

Just wanted to thank you for your time last week and the opportunity you have presented to my company.

It was a real pleasure meeting you. As promised, I will get a proposal over to you by X date and I will be sending you the two references.

As mentioned, you will be sending me a, b and c.

In the meantime, here are a couple of testimonials from our clients about our company:

[Insert one or two testimonials from ideally a similar company to them with a similar challenge that you have been able to solve.]

I look forward to speaking with you on X date, to agree on next steps. If you or the team have any further questions, please feel free to call.

Have a great rest of your week.

Warmest regards,

Tony

I send the following email to thank the client for the business. I prefer sending the client a thank you card, as it's even more personal; however, as plan B, this is a nice touch:

Dear NAME,

I want to thank you for putting your trust in me and my company to deliver.

Our objective is simple – to exceed your expectations at every step of the process, so we can build a fantastic partnership for years to come.

Warmest regards,

Tony

My recommendation is that if you find yourself having to write out an email a second time, then that needs to be saved as a template. There are two ways to go about this. First, you can use your signature to create the different templates, so when you decide which template is required, you select which signature that is linked with. Alternatively, create a series of folders in your sent folder for the various emails – that is, 'have I offended you' folder – and then go to your sent items, find the email and drag it into the right folder.

5
Preparation

'My team, the Green Bay Packers, never lost a football game; they just ran out of time'.

—Vince Lombardi

Why are some people more successful than others? Why does Novak Djokovic either win every tennis tournament he enters or gets into the final on a bad day? Surely he's just naturally gifted, you might think. The closest thing this guy is to a robot, and, arguably, the best tennis player ever to have graced the courts. But he still has a coach, practices every single day and sticks to a routine religiously before every game he plays. He watches more games of his opponents than any other player in the circuit. He knows his opponents' strengths and weaknesses, as well as his own.

How many times have you phoned your direct competitors posing as a customer to see how they deal with you? This is a great way of learning their line of questioning that you could bring into your sales pattern. How many proposals have you obtained from your competitors? Again, this will enable you to take the best bits from each and amalgamate them into the best proposal. This will surely put you in the strongest position to be successful in a proposal-only situation, where the prospect wishes to see something before they commit to a meeting.

How would you describe Novak Djokovic in one word? Champion, winner, rich, successful, ambitious – there are many more adjectives to illustrate the genius, however, the word 'professional' encapsulates them all.

As a professional salesperson, preparation is par for the course. Imagine the following scenario:

Person A is about to smart call a prospect (this is cold calling done smartly), as they feel they can help them. They have been on their website for three minutes and have a rough idea about what the company does, and therefore can start to create an angle, in terms of what they can do for them. They have clients whom they have helped previously similar to the prospective customer, so they are ready to build immediate credibility and value.

Person B picks up the phone and makes a call.

Who do you think is the most likely to be successful?

If you were the only person calling these prospective customers, then maybe homework isn't required. However, in this competitive and forever-changing marketplace, you always need to be one step ahead of your competition.

Do you ever have conversations where you return from work and your partner or your family asks you, 'How was your day?' and you think to yourself, '*the same as yesterday, and the day before*'. Those conversations used to bore me, and I thought, '*How do I avoid this demotivated feeling?*' I realised that if I apply the same mindset in the gym as to when I'm in the office, it will become more fun and competitive.

I remember starting the gym at the age of 21. The trainer showed me all the equipment and had set for me a programme to help me achieve my goals of toning up. I could bench 35 kg, which at the time seemed a great achievement, except when the beef cake after me put a further 100 kg on each side of the bar and began his warm up!

By the time I reached 23, I was benching 60 kg and attempted a further kilogram on the bar every time I went. When I finally achieved it, the feeling was euphoric and I could not wait to get back to the gym and beat 65 kg.

I began to apply the same logic to work. I set myself specific goals every day I was in the office making sales calls. To begin, I would strive to make more calls than the day before. I would monitor how many pitches I made, and set myself goals to the number of qualified meetings I could generate.

This is not only motivational but also identifies which areas need further development.

Date	Calls	DMC (Decision-Maker Contacted)	Pitch	Meeting	Quotes
1/5/22	100	10	8	2	0

As you can see from the table, on making 100 calls in a day, I only managed to get hold of 10 people who I identified as the key decision-makers and who would be worth meeting. Two of them were busy and with eight of them I had an enjoyable conversation and could get my pitch across. My result was two qualified meetings and no quotes.

Now, many salespeople would look at those figures and think they were converting at 2%; they make 100 calls and only achieve two meetings and can become quite demotivated. But the true conversion rate is 25%; eight pitches and two meetings. There is clearly a lot of room for improvement, yet much better than 2%.

These figures give the salesperson a lot of information. Why were only 10% of your calls speaking to decision-makers? This makes you look closer at the leads you were using and target more effectively.

Why did you only manage to convert 25% of your pitches into a qualified meeting? What happened to the other 75%?

Why out of the six decision-makers who sold you the reason won't meet you, and what were the reasons you were unable to create an opportunity to quote them?

To monitor your development, I would suggest keeping a record of your daily figures in an Excel spreadsheet, which can highlight many trends as follows:

Date	Calls	DMC	Pitch	Meeting	Quote
01/02/2022	100	10	8	2	0
02/02/2022	76	8	7	1	1
03/02/2022	79	7	4	2	1
04/02/2022	86	5	3	1	1
05/02/2022	91	7	5	2	0
Total	432	37	27	8	3

At the end of the week, tally your figures for the five different sections. At the end of the month, tally the four or five weeks of calls you made. You can then calculate your averages across all five sections. If you do this consistently, and do not use this call sheet as a 'cheat sheet' and add more numbers in it to make yourself feel better then you'll start to see real trends.

By truly understanding your numbers, you can start to set goals based on accurate figures and can reverse engineer things. As an example, if you learn that your average conversion from pitch to meeting is 50%, that is, for every four pitches that you make, you'll book two meetings, then you can work out the number of pitches you need to aim for to achieve your desired number of meetings. If my goal is to book three meetings every day, then I need to be getting six pitches in a day. I can then calculate how many calls I need to make to establish how many decision-makers I am likely to reach.

Therefore, rather than crossing your fingers at the beginning of your day and hoping you'll book three meetings, you can plan for it accordingly. There are other benefits to knowing your numbers to this level, which I will expand on later in this book in the motivation chapter.

Remember, 'hoping' is not a strategy. There's a saying in sales management, 'If you can't measure it, you cannot manage it'. As a sales manager, you must know your sales teams' numbers, otherwise it becomes very challenging to know which areas to focus on with each member of your team.

People say in sales you need to be 'money hungry'. I disagree with this theory, I feel you need to be driven, tenacious and have a hunger to succeed. But people have different motivations.

My wife was in sales, and she was remarkably successful. Commission was irrelevant to her. If she got a pat on her back by her boss at the end of the week it meant the world to her. After three consecutive months of being the top sales performer, she was given a hand-written letter by the MD of the company. I am not exaggerating when I say that she came home skipping with a smile on her face like a Cheshire cat. I thought she'd won the lottery.

We have a client who has an inbound call centre with 60 operatives taking calls. One of the areas that the client wanted help with was to improve the morale. We bought a trophy that couldn't have cost more than £10, but the boss had the top performer of the week knocking at his door on a Friday night demanding the trophy before going home. This clearly shows different things motivate different people, and as a manager it's part of your job to know what motivates each member of your team.

Whether you sell over the phone, virtually or face-to-face depends on what product or service you sell and your role in sales. There are other criteria that will play a part, such as the average order value, the length of the sales cycle and so on. Salespeople who start their sales journey on the phone need to consider their 'G.A.P' to prepare successfully for every call.

Preparation for a Call

G in G.A.P. is the goal. It was the late Richard Denny who said, 'If you don't have a goal, you cannot score'. So, when you pick up a phone, think what are you aiming for? When I make a sales call to a prospect, I always set two goals. The reason is that if I don't achieve the first goal, which I call my primary goal, then I can look to achieve my secondary goal. This goes back to the positive mindset I spoke about earlier.

When I ask most salespeople, 'What are you looking to achieve from the call?' They'll often say, 'To have a good conversation'. I would say that this is necessary, but it's not a goal. The question is what do you want to happen as a result of a good conversation? Then they arrive at the answer – a well-qualified meeting with the key decision-makers or stakeholders.

Then the question is, if you don't manage to book a meeting with the key decision-makers or stakeholders, what would be another goal that you'd be happy with?

They say, 'Names of alternative contacts, mobile numbers, information on the current solution they use, renewal date and so on'. This becomes the 'secondary goal'.

When I coach sales teams, whose role is to make outbound calls all day, they have days where they get no appointments. You can see at the end of the day, they look deflated, frustrated, cheesed off and have negative body language. I ask how their day went and I get vomited on with negativity – worst day ever, should have taken a day off, total waste of my time, no one was available to speak. Once they get all of that off their chests, I ask a few more questions?

How many people did you speak with? Fifty-six.

How many decision-makers did you find out? Thirty-four.

How many direct lines or mobile numbers did you get? Fourteen.

So, when you started making your first sales call today at 08:45 am, how many of those 34 decision-makers' names did you have? Zero.

And how many of those 14 mobile numbers did you have? None.

So then you had a fantastic day, you're just choosing to not focus on it. The salesperson then gives me an evil and confused stare and says, 'But I set a goal of two meetings and I got zero'. Correct, but rather than focusing on what 'you did not get', that is, no meetings, focus on what you did get, 34 decision-makers' names and 14 mobile numbers. You have now increased the probability of getting hold of them over the next four days. Therefore, it wasn't a waste of your time, it was a waste of energy spent focusing on the things you did not achieve.

A in G.A.P. is the approach. This is an area so many salespeople get so wrong. When making a sales call, what's one thing that you can guarantee from the prospects' side? They are going to be busy. They will be busy in a meeting, preparing for a meeting or busy at work, therefore, we are interrupting them no matter what.

Therefore, if we are interrupting them, we need to make sure that we make it a positive interruption. An interruption that the prospect is happy to take. So, when preparing for that call, it's imperative that all you are thinking about is W.I.I.F.M:

What's in It for Me?

The 'me' being the prospect. What I mean by 'what's in it for me?' is what am I getting out of this call.

For this approach, you need to think about your 'elevator pitch'. Imagine you are in an elevator and your ideal prospect walks in and asks, 'What do you do?' You now have 10 to 15 seconds to say something that will engage, inspire and entice that person to say, 'That sounds interesting, tell me more'.

So when preparing your elevator pitch or whatever you wish to call it, there are a few things you need to think about to achieve your desired effect. I got a cold call recently from a gentleman trying to sell marketing programmes for my sales training company; his tone of voice was good and he sounded enthusiastic, however the message was irrelevant to me. He told me that his company had been established for 27 years (irrelevant to me), he told me that they specialise in digital marketing programmes (irrelevant to me) and that he had worked with other sales training companies such as A and B (this was the only thing that caught my attention).

Although what he failed to tell me, which would have been the most important piece of information to me, is how he helped the other sales training companies. The end result is all that I and other business owners want to hear, and without this information, it's all irrelevant.

P in G.A.P. is preparation. There are a few stages for preparing for your call.

1. Goal

Like we discussed only a moment ago, if your primary goal is to make an appointment with the decision-maker, then you need to prepare at least two dates that you're available to meet that person(s).

2. Know their market

You need to understand what the company you are calling does. Now, I am not suggesting you to do a 15-minutes research, because you could end up leaving a voice mail, which would not be the most productive use of your time; however, you need to look at their website for at least a minute to grasp what they do. You need to look at their social media channels to see what things you can learn about them.

Then look at your clients that you have already worked with and are similar to them; either competitors of them or would have similar requirements as them.

3. Talk results

This is by far the most important stage of the opening statement. When making the sales call, do NOT talk about what you do, instead talk about what you have done, successfully, with companies or people like them. Remember, people only care about how you can help their business, so the result is everything. So, look at the clients you have worked with, who are similar to them and then make a note of the results you have achieved for them.

The A–Z of Success

In my business, we call this our 'A–Z of success'. To help save my sales team's time and equip them with the information they need when making a call, we have created the following document. Although it can be time consuming to create, and it is an ever-evolving document, it will make a significant difference to your sales team's probability of converting the call to an appointment or a sale, depending on their primary goal of the call. We have broken down every industry we have worked in, and the different companies within the industry. We have looked at the product/service we sold the company and, most importantly, the result we helped our client achieve.

Industry	Client	Product	Result
Automotive	Select Car Leasing	Inbound training	Increased conversion by 14%
	BMW	Retail training	Increased AOV by 6%
Banking	UBS BNP Paribas	Account management Leadership training	Reduced attrition by 11% and improved sales' teams morale
Call centres	Oceans Connect	Inbound training	Increased conversion by 8%
	Hammonds Furniture	Inbound training	Increased conversion by 14% and AOV by 6%
Data room	Imprima	Telesales Training	Tripled their appointments

Once your sales' teams are armed with their A to Z, they feel more comfortable going into a call. So, when they get hold of the stakeholder, with confidence, they are able to share who they have helped and, most importantly, how they have helped.

Your first question

Once you have delivered your opening statement, you need to get the prospect talking; the only way to do that is by asking a well-planned open question that will engage him or her. You need to therefore think about the information you would like to obtain, whilst ensuring it's going to create a need for your product or service.

The first question you ask should focus on the biggest problem you believe the prospect is currently navigating. This is known as a leading question, as you are leading the prospect to share what you want them to.

Write and rehearse

This is the second, most important stage of the opening statement. You need to write it down and practice it, and rehearse it out aloud at least five times so that it flows and sounds natural and not scripted.

Let me show you an example of an opening statement I would use while calling an estate agent to create an opportunity for me to deliver sales training.

1. Objective

When calling an estate agent, my goal is to make a qualified appointment with the decision-maker. Due to my success within this industry, I am aware the decision-makers are the owners or the MDs of the estate agency.

2. Know their market

I would carry out some brief research and find out if the estate agent who I am calling does both sales and lettings. I would be aware of the number of branches they have, an approximate size of their team and the areas they cover. I would then look through my A–Z of success to see the estate agents that I have already trained and that do both sales and lettings and have a similar number of branches as the one I am calling. The reason my existing client needs to be like the estate agency I am calling is to build credibility. I need to demonstrate that I have helped other estate and letting agents with a similar number of branches within a similar geographic area. The reason is, if they had two branches and were based in London and I talk about an estate agency I have helped in Newcastle (six hours away by car) with 23 offices, they would argue that I do not understand their business and/or market.

Now, if I had not helped an estate and letting agency similar to them, I would not lie. This would discredit my company immediately and could ruin my reputation. Therefore, I would look for an example where I have helped an estate agency that had a similar challenge to them and explain how I helped them overcome it.

3. Talk results

Due to my success in the industry, I am aware of some key challenges estate agencies currently face. Their biggest challenge in today's market is a lack of instructions (properties) to sell or to let. In addition, they are constantly being pushed on their fees. Therefore, I need to demonstrate within the first 15 to 20 seconds that I have helped an estate agency like them to overcome these challenges.

4. Your first question

As I know that lack of stock to rent is a major issue with many estate agents I train, I will create a question that will highlight this problem as I have a solution up my sleeve. Now this is what I would say:

'Good morning John (always use their first name and avoid Sir or madam), thanks for taking my call'. Notice I do not ask if it is convenient to speak, as it gives them an opportunity to say no. If you don't want to hear a no, do not ask a question that allows them to say no.

'My name is Tony Morris, and I am the founder of TMI. Are you familiar with my business?'

Yes – 'Great as you are probably aware. . .'

OR

No – 'Okay, to make you aware. . .'

'We have been successfully helping many estate agents such as (name drop ones they'd have heard of and are similar to) by helping them double their instructions, without spending an extra penny on marketing'.

This statement will create curiosity and provoke a conversation. Remember, the objective is to engage your prospect and get them talking, ideally 80% of the conversation.

'At this stage, I don't know if we can help you as well, so can you help me by telling me. . .'.

(This is a good take away phrase, as you are not guaranteeing whether you can help them, however it's allowing you to ask some questions to see if you can).

Now, we ask a question that is directly aimed at the problem that you've helped estate agencies like them to overcome.

It's worth noting at this point that it's more impactful to focus the conversation on the problems that you solve. There are only two reasons people buy anything – to gain pleasure or avoid pain. Psychologists have told us that people are four times more motivated to solve a problem than to achieve a goal. Therefore, the conversation should always focus on avoiding or solving pain or problems, rather than gaining pleasure or achieving a goal.

My first question would be, 'How are you proactively increasing your instructions without having to increase your marketing spend?'

This is a great open question to get them talking about a problem I am confident they have. They are likely to respond with, 'We are doing a, b and c, although not achieving the desired results'. As I created curiosity in my opening statement, they are likely to ask me, 'How do you help agents double their instructions?' Rather than giving my secret away, I would respond with, 'That is the first thing I will share in a meeting with you'. This is very assumptive; however, I have enticed the prospect to a meeting, as they will be eager to find out my secret.

I would then say, 'To ensure I can help you, I have a few other questions for you'. Again, this enables me to ask some qualifying questions to ascertain key information and to make sure the meeting is the best use of my time. My questions would be the following:

'Tell me about the size of your team and their roles and responsibilities'.

'Tell me what tasks are working for you and which ones are not'.

'Explain to me how your team looks to build value, so they do not have to drop their fees to secure the instruction'.

In his book, *Spin Selling*, Neil Rackham shares his four-stage methodology:

Situation – Understand the prospects' current situation. This can include the size of the team, the tasks they undertake, the system and processes they currently use and so on.

I would then move to the second stage of Neil Rackham's methodology:

Pain – In addition to a lack of instructions, tell me the two biggest challenges you are currently facing? This is an intelligent leading question, as I am leading the prospect to focus on the pain that the prospect is facing.

What is preventing your team from commanding the fees you need as a business?

Once the prospect has opened about the pain and problems they are facing as an agency, you move into the third stage, the **Implication** questions as follows:

If you do not start getting the number of instructions you need, what do you see are the implications of this? This question starts to make the problem even bigger and the pain even worse. You then keep building on this pain by asking more probing questions; if your fees levels keep dropping, what is your back up plan?

This moves you nicely to the fourth and final stage of Neil Rackham's S.P.I.N methodology, **need/payoff** questions. This is where you start to ask questions to lead into the solution. In the example of the estate and letting agency, I would ask the following: So, if we were able to help your agency to triple your valuation in the next three weeks, how many instructions (properties) would you anticipate your team winning?

And if we showed your team how to build value and differentiate them from all your competition, and they were able to command double the fees of your cheapest competitors, what would that look like financially for your business?

Once you start hitting those numbers, what would that enable you to do to grow your business?

Therefore, engaging the prospect and getting them to open up and share information enables you to use that information wisely to uncover the pain they're experiencing. Following the S.P.I.N methodology will help you build your pitch on the pain, to make it a priority for the decision-maker and to do something about it. It's then a case of recommending your solution and clearly explaining how you can help solve their problems.

Let me show you an example of an opening gambit that I created for a client of mine who sells promotional merchandise, that is, branded products.

Goal. Book a qualified meeting with the key decision-maker(s).

Approach was as follows:

'Good morning John, thanks for taking my call. My name is Tony Morris from (company).

Have you heard of us before?'

Yes – 'Great, as you already might know. . .'

No – 'Okay, to make you aware. . .'

'We specialise in offering creative solutions for your promotional needs to increase your client base and gain brand awareness'.

To see if we can help you, tell me. . .

Which promotional merchandise have you used in the past?

What were your objectives when using this merchandise?

What results did you achieve from it?

Based on what you have kindly shared, I am confident we can help you select the right merchandise that will be tailored to the right audience, which will help your sales team by warming up the prospect before they make a sales call.

It makes sense to arrange a meeting to get a deeper understanding of your business and understand your ideal client, and then we can make our recommendations.

If you decide to work with us, aside from you, who else would be involved in the decision? (This is a vital question, as you want to try and get all decision-makers to attend the meeting).

Great, it's important we meet you both, as we often find business partners ask different questions and we want to answer those, so together you can make an informed decision. (This is called a 'justification statement,' as you're justifying why both decision-makers need to attend the meeting).

Looking at my diary, I am available tomorrow at 11:45 a.m. or Friday at 15:15; what time suits you both better?

There are a few techniques in this question as follows:

The first technique is called, 'don't ask, tell'. I wasn't asking the prospect if they'd like to meet, I was asking which of the two options suit them best.

The second technique is the alternative close. By presenting two options, the prospect is going to select one of them. You will find 80% of people choose the second option. This is called recency; the last thing they heard. Try this with your friends, when they next come around for a take away. If you want Chinese say, 'Shall we get Indian or Chinese tonight?, You will get Chinese. This does not always work. I often say to my wife, shall we go to the cinema or just stay in and have sex? I have seen so many films, I could become a film critic.

The third and final technique is called psychological numbers. By saying, 11:45 a.m. or 15:15, you are implying that you're busy the other time, and it looks good to show you're busy. It's the same as 97p is cheaper than £1. So when you book meetings, do not do it on the hour.

Now that you have used the G.A.P. method, you will have many meetings booked in your diary. They may be a combination of virtual and face-to-face meetings. To increase your probability of a successful outcome, you need to prepare for the meeting.

Prepare for a Meeting

Before attending a meeting, you need to decide what you want to happen as a result of that meeting. I would suggest having two goals, a primary and a secondary. This could be as simple as winning the business, however it's not always that simple. When I sold software, my prospects normally needed to put the software on trial to make sure the 'user' liked all the features it had to offer. Please note that the 'decision-makers' were NOT the 'users', therefore both the parties were needed to be satisfied to win the business. This involved getting them set up to test it, ensuring they understood the trial process and understanding their expectations.

If my primary goal is to win the business and it transpires that not all the decision-makers are present, then my goal changes. I would need to ensure that I get buy-in from those present and eliminate any concerns they may have. I would then get a commitment to set up a second meeting with all the parties present.

Once you know your goal, there is certain information you will need to ascertain to recommend the right product or service to the customer and achieve your goal. I would recommend writing a list of all the information you want to ascertain and then in your meeting book, write a list of open questions, which will help direct the conversation to gain this information.

When I arrive at a face-to-face meeting I make sure that when I open my meeting book, the prospective customer sees the print out I have of their company website. This shows them that I've done some homework and have invested time and energy in preparing for the meeting, which shows that I'm hungry to work with them.

I will always visit the prospective customers' website and prepare two to three questions about things that I've seen, again to show interest and to demonstrate that I've spent time researching about them. Make the questions interesting and relevant to what you're there to help them with. For my business, if I see a company has previously won an award for sales, I would say 'I noticed that you won the award for best sales in the Southeast region; what are you doing to retain that award this year?'

Always search for all the people you're meeting on LinkedIn prior to the meeting. Again it shows an interest in them and you can see if you know any of their connections. You can use this as a good ice breaker, and if you've helped someone they trust this can only help you.

Make sure you are dressed appropriately. It's important to find the dress code of the company you're meeting and then dress the same. Some of my clients will dress smart casual and wear chinos and a shirt and blazer, others will wear a suit, shirt and tie. If you visit their website and look at their 'meet the team' page, this can often give you an indication of how they like to dress. If in doubt, always dress smart.

You must ensure that you have all the resources with you. Think through everything the prospective customer may ask to see and bring it along. Business cards, pen and notebook are a given, however there will be other things that are not so obvious.

If you're conducting a meeting and you know there are a few people attending, I would recommend emailing them all prior to the meeting to introduce yourself. If you only have one point of contact, ask them, 'Are other people going to be joining us for the meeting?' and if they are, then say, 'It would be really helpful if I can email them all prior to the meeting, so I can find out what one thing is important to them and ensure that I bring that information along to our meeting. Please can I have their names and emails?' In the book, *Influence* by Dr Robert Cialdini, its proven that if you justify the reason you want to do something, prior to asking the question, you are much more likely to get what you want. If you just ask, 'Can I have the email addresses of the people that will be attending the meeting?' Your contact will most likely say, 'It's okay, you can just email me'.

There are two ways to ask if others will be attending the meeting. The one I just mentioned, 'Are other people going to be joining us for the meeting?' and the following, 'If we end up working together, aside from you, who else will be involved in deciding the right option for your company?' If you ask outright, 'Are you the decision-maker', it could make them feel bad if they are not, and their answer may not be accurate.

A good example of this is, I was speaking to the MD of the largest online H&S company in the United Kingdom. When I booked the meeting, I asked him, 'As the MD, I assume this will be your decision?' He replied, 'Yes of course'. I drove two hours to arrive at the meeting and we had a great meeting for about one and a half hours. At the end of the meeting, I asked, 'What are the next steps to arrange the training?', a nice assumptive close. He replied, 'Well I would need to discuss this with my business partner'. 'Business partner', I had asked him if it was his decision and he said yes I thought to myself. Whose fault was this? Mine. I asked the wrong question. He was not lying to me, as it was his decision, however he was just one of the decision-makers.

So, once you know who all will be involved in the decision-making, one vital question to ask them all in that email is 'So I am best prepared for our meeting, what specifically are you looking to get out of our meeting?' If your competition doesn't ask this, it already puts you one step ahead and enables you to prepare effectively, ensuring everyone gets what they want out of their time with you.

It's inevitable that the prospect will raise objections during the meeting, so your job is to prepare for them. I always recommend writing a list of objections that you think they might raise and then have the response ready. This will prevent you from being caught out in the meeting.

Finally, you need to get in the right state of mind before the meeting. On my podcast, *Confessions of a Serial Seller*, I asked the guest, 'What strategies do they use to get into the right state of mind before a sales call and or a meeting?' Following are just some of the strategies they shared with me:

Strategy 1: They listen to uplifting music on their journey, which motivates them and helps them feel like they can achieve anything.

Strategy 2: They listen to an Audible book on their journey so that they can constantly learn ideas, which they might be able to use on the call or in the meeting.

Strategy 3: The goals that they write are written as if they have already won them. Rather than using the language like, 'If I win the business, then I will hit my target'. They write down, 'Now that I have won this piece of business, I am on the way to exceeding my target again'. Writing it this way helps you visualise the right outcome, which tricks your subconscious mind into believing that you have already achieved it.

Strategy 4: They repeat positive affirmations to themselves. Such as, 'I am the best sales professional they will ever meet. My product, service and solution are the best in the marketplace and nothing comes close to what I offer'.

Strategy 5: They go through the call or meeting in their head, which makes them feel super prepared for the things that may arise.

The truth is that you can use any of these strategies that works for you; the key point is that all the top sales professionals in the world use one.

6
My Best Sales Lesson Yet

'Winners never quit; quitters never win'.

—Vince Lombardi

One of the best lessons in my sales career to date was when I was selling address management software. When you enter your postcode on a website, this is the software that fills out your full address. It also cleansed millions of data records and was used in all the major call centres and other big businesses all over the UK.

I was driving home from a day of meetings and my mobile rang at about 16:30 pm, a call from my office. It was our receptionist, Karen, who said, 'I have a PA on the phone from a company that wants some "information" on our data capture software; it sounds like a complete waste. Shall I just take a message?'

If I'm honest, I couldn't be bothered to take the call and was inclined to agree with Karen. I thought, it was just a PA, and not a decision-maker or an influencer; they are simply looking for information. *I have software to sell, and if they want information, they should look at our website or visit the library.* I had never heard of the company before, so it was clearly a tinpot Mickey Mouse operation. But I reluctantly told Karen 'to keep her on hold'. I pulled over into an Esso petrol station in Highgate, got out my notebook, a pen and my diary and was as ready as I'd ever be. The call went something like this:

PA: Hi there, my name is Louise and I'm calling on behalf of Ian Higgins, the Global IT Director of XXX, and we need some data capture and data cleansing software for our 300-seat call centres in Bracknell. We were wondering if you could help.

ME: As I was busy calculating how much money this deal could actually be worth, I managed to get the words out, 'Of course, I can help. I would recommend I come and see you and Ian, and find out much more about your setup and your specific requirements'.

PA: That would be ideal; could you come tomorrow? I know Ian wants to get on with this pretty sharpish.

The meeting was organized for 10 a.m. the following day.

Lesson 1: Never prejudge a situation, as you never know how big an opportunity could be. I now treat every single call the same, no matter from which company they are calling or for what they are asking. Remember, they may be looking to spend £50 with you, which in commission will earn you tuppence, but who do they know? Treat them well and you could get the referral of a lifetime.

Lesson 2: Never listen to Karen.

I awoke at 6:15 a.m., as by looking at a route planner, it was 68 miles to Bracknell, and Karen said it would take an hour to get there, so I gave myself two hours. I wanted to spend a good hour looking through my potential client's website, familiarising myself with the various parts of their business and exactly what they do.

My previous knowledge was that they were a bank and are French, but I wouldn't bet my life on it. After looking through about 20 pages on their site and writing out about eight questions in my meeting book, I checked I had everything in my work case; the software itself, my laptop and adapter, business cards and a working pen. I had printed out a copy of their home page, which would be visible when I opened my notebook to show I had done my home-work. I put on my best suit, shirt and tie, as they say, 'How you look on the outside is an exact reflection of how you feel on the inside'. I polished my shoes and was ready for action.

I remember vividly, the first meeting was with Louise and Ian. Ian was a real 'techie' and asked loads of complex questions about how the software would integrate with their system and what code it was built in, Linux or blah, blah, blah and what flavour of Linux.

Just to clarify my technical expertise, I am very good at turning on a laptop and I like looking at pictures and I can send emails, that's it as far as it goes. My manager at that time, a guy called Greg, said, 'To impress the prospective customer about your technical knowledge, ask the following questions: "On what platform of Windows do you operate?" "What APIs would you use to integrate into your system?"' But when I asked Ian these two questions, his eyes lit up and he replied, 'Windows NT version 8.2 and it uses Linux language'. I almost crapped myself and rude words were going through my mind about Greg, as Ian began to fire these technical questions at me. I had to explain that I am almost Amish in my technical knowledge and my objective of the meeting was to gain an understanding of his specific requirements, then I would bring along my technical director to go through the finer detail about the actual software.

Lesson 3: If you are lacking knowledge in a certain area, do not expose that weakness by asking questions regarding that area.

Lesson 4: Never listen to Greg.

In the meeting, I managed to ascertain a lot of information about their setup and the issues that were arising in the call centre, regarding down time and speed of response. By doing this, not only was I highlighting the need, but by asking problem questions, it was helping me make the issues worse than Ian first thought. This naturally built the value of my offering and developed the need even further. These problem questions were taught to me from a fantastic sales book called *SPIN Selling* by Neil Rackham, which I would strongly recommend if you sell any type of IT solution.

I noticed Louise was making notes in the meeting yet remaining very quiet. So, I got her involved and asked about her background and her remit at XXX. She said, 'I'm Ian's PA and pretty much run his work life, organise his meetings, etc.'. She also mentioned she helps the call centre manager on occasions with purchasing equipment and dealing with any problems, etc. After about an hour and a half, we wrapped up the meeting and I said, 'I would go away and put a proposal together, then come back with my technical director to go through the techie stuff and run through the proposal face to face'.

We got out our diaries and the second meeting was made. If you know a follow-up meeting is needed rather than a phone call, always arrange that when you are with the prospect. This clearly shows a level of commitment from their end, and you don't have to worry about chasing them afterwards.

Lesson 5: If there is more than one person in a meeting, make sure to include them in the conversation somehow or other.

I lost a very big deal with my training company because there were three directors, a senior sales manager and a PA in the meeting. I didn't completely ignore the PA, but I probably didn't say more than 10 words to her in the meeting, as I didn't feel she played any real relevance to the discussions. When I got the email to say I'd lost the business, they said 'Sam, the PA, didn't warm to me and she was unsure if I would have fitted in with the sales team'.

Apparently after meeting three other training companies, they all had an equal part in recommending which one to choose. An expensive lesson to learn, but a good one nonetheless. After my second and third meeting with Ian, the call centre manager and their IT Director, we started to make real progress with XXX. They told me all along I was up against our biggest competitor, who I knew were similarly priced to ours and had a very similar offering. Both solutions had the same capabilities at the end of the day; we may have just wrapped it up slightly differently.

We were about four months into the sales cycle and the final test was the software trial. I went back to Basingstoke with my technical director whose first language was 'techie talk'. You couldn't let him speak to the customer because not only would he scare them, but he would 100% lose the opportunity for me. I had to brief him very strictly that he could only speak when spoken to, and was to answer their technical questions only. He wasn't a personable guy, so anything that came out of his mouth sounded condescending, rude and obnoxious. To give you some idea, he was 47 years old and still lived at home with his mum. I am not judging, but it was a little odd.

We set them up for a 30-day trial of the software, and I had arranged to return for my fourth and final meeting to gain their feedback and hopefully do the business. At the end of that time, I knew what their expectation of the trial was, I knew they were testing it against our competition, and in my knowledge, I had done everything I could to get the business. We had set key criteria to trial the software against, in terms of, speed, outcome, volumes of data it could handle, etc.

Over the next month, I went through our pricing structure with Ian for the software licences, as they required a server licence to cover all 300 users of our solution. This was the most expensive licence we offered, and we were looking at approximately £250,000 over a five-year licensing agreement. Although this sounds like a huge amount and, for me at the age of 23, it was the biggest deal I had been involved in, I only earn commission on the one-year licence. The MD of the company made a commercial decision to not pay the sales team on retaining their client, which, as you can imagine, caused numerous sales meeting debates, but it led to the same inevitable outcome, like it or lump it.

I returned, at the agreed time, to their head office in Basingstoke alone to get feedback on the trial and to potentially do the deal. I had the contract in my case, and I was ready to do business. As I entered the building, there were six salespeople sitting patiently in reception with their badges on, clearly displaying the name of my competition. They all stared at me and knew exactly who I was. We all knew today was D-Day, and the competition was on. I went into the boardroom, where I met Ian and Louise again and sat down to discuss their findings.

The feedback on our software was brilliant. It exceeded their expectations and did exactly what they needed. They felt there wasn't a significant difference between our solution and my competition. So, it came down to price and their gut feeling. They didn't want to share my competition's exact prices; all they said was that I was coming in more and they wanted to discuss if there was any movement on my price.

I said, 'Putting the price to one side, what else would be important to you?' They explained the structure of the licensing agreement and the ongoing technical support plays a big factor in the deal. I justified the reason for my price and explained why I couldn't move on it; however, I agreed that rather than paying £75,000 in year 1 and £43,750 for the further four years, we agreed to do £50,000 per year for the next five years, and a two-hour IT support resource per week. Ian and Louise said they wanted to sit down with the competition and then would be calling me later today to give me their decision'.

Lesson 6: When up against a competitor and it comes down to price, don't be scared of sticking to your guns.

By asking a good question, I was able to identify two other factors that were important to them, which enabled me to keep my prices and not lose any gross profit for my business.

It was only about four hours later when I got the call, although it felt like about a month. I was the most nervous and anxious I'd ever been. 'We want to go with you, Tony', Ian said.

I almost screamed with excitement and thanked him so much for his business and reassured him I wouldn't let him down. As I am always looking for feedback, I asked what reasons he had for choosing us over the competition.

He said, 'It came down to one thing, we preferred you and bought into you throughout the five-month process'. Ecstatic and overjoyed, I thanked him again and immediately phoned my boss.

The following day, contracts were signed, the licence fees were set up and all the administration was dealt with. I had already worked out before the deal was signed that I was making £9300 commission, and for a 23-year-old that was a fantastic month and by far the best I'd ever had.

The following month, I carried on with my business and got back to the other deals in my pipeline. I received a couple of calls from the IT director at XXX and simply answered his questions where

I could and then transferred him to my IT support team when I was unable to help.

I came into the office on the Monday morning and as I was sipping my tea and discussing the weekend sports results with my fellow sales team, I worked my way through the 26 emails in my inbox. Marked in red for high priority was an email from Ian Higgins from XXX.

I opened the email and didn't get much further than the third line that read: *We have decided to cancel our contract with you and are aware that today is our 29th day into our 30-day cancellation period.*

I really had to control the sudden urge to throw up all over my computer screen and just shouted obscenities until my boss came over to look at what I was reading. As I managed to compose myself and read my way through the email, Ian explained he felt part of our offering was a huge business dataset, inclusive with the software. My boss and I got to that part of the email at the same time, as he shouted at me in an accusing tone, 'Did you offer that as part of the deal?'

'Absolutely not', I responded, and it was genuinely the first I'd ever heard of it. My boss's parting words in front of the entire sales floor of 18 people were 'If you lose this deal, you are in serious shit'.

Lesson 7: When you become a manager, treat your team the exact opposite to how Dave treated us.

I would describe him as David Brent from *The Office*, without any of the humour. In all seriousness, in my entire sales career David taught me the most about management, in terms of how not to do it. Although he was as motivational as a crack addict, his awful style of management did highlight the real 'no-nos' in how to motivate, inspire and manage a sales force.

Before calling Ian, I wanted to be best prepared for the call. I spent the next two hours going through every single email correspondence that was ever emailed to one another and to anyone else within his business.

Fortunately, I had filed all of the emails away in a XXX folder in my outlook. There was no mention anywhere of this dataset that he claimed was part of our agreement. I had a meeting with my boss, David, and the MD of my company to discuss how to tackle it. The MD, Terry, felt I should call Ian and find out when this dataset was mentioned and where it was written as part of the deal. Terry explained the dataset was worth around £4500 to us as a business, so in worst case scenario I would have to concede and offer the dataset and take the £4,500 out of my commission package. Although it would hurt, losing £9,800 would hurt more, and I'd rather have 50% of something than 100% of nothing.

TONY: Good morning, Ian, Tony here. I just received your email and am both shocked and confused.

IAN: Well, it's very simple in our eyes. We made it crystal clear that this B2B (business to business) dataset was part of the overall package and now we have received all the software licences, and it wasn't included.

TONY: Okay, I am sorry for the confusion. I have looked through every single email correspondence between us and there is no mention of this dataset anywhere.

IAN: That may be so, but it was discussed in our meeting and Louise recalls the conversation as well. Without this, you leave us with no choice but to cancel and go with your competitor.

TONY: Okay, clearly, I don't want it to get to that and I am sure we can organise something to come to a compromise.

IAN: Without this dataset, there is no compromise, Tony.

TONY: I value your business so what I am prepared to do is give you the dataset at no cost to you and I'll personally bear the costs, as there has clearly been a miscommunication somewhere down the line.

IAN: I am not happy with that. The fact you have got this wrong so early on in our business relationship concerns me, and I have lost faith and confidence in you as a person. I need to go away and really consider this. I will get back to you when I'm ready.

I genuinely could have cried and if I wasn't surrounded by my strong team of 18 sales guys, I would have sobbed like a six-year-old girl who had lost her Barbie doll. I went and fed this back to Dave and Terry, who were both furious with me and asked to be kept updated.

I got the call that I dreaded about three hours later. Ian said, 'I regret to inform you that we have decided to go with your competitor and there is nothing you can say or do that will persuade us otherwise'.

To this day, I never found out the real reason I lost this deal. My gut feeling is my competition went back in and dropped their pants and halved their prices, and Ian was happy to accept. I know the dataset was just his get-out clause as I didn't even know it was something we could have offered, so therefore it was an impossibility I would have discussed it. However, what can I learn from this costly and soul-destroying experience?

Lesson 8: Always write down absolutely every minute detail of what you have agreed to with the client in your contract. Get the client to read it and sign off to acknowledge full understanding and agreement. You must also accept the biggest sales lesson of all; you can't win them all and sometimes if you look back and you know you did everything right, it can be a lack of morals from the customer that caused the cancellation. Get over it and move on!

7
Motivation

'You can have everything in life you want by simply helping people get what they want'.

—Zig Ziglar

Motivation is what drives us every single day. It's what gets us up in the morning to work five days a week, and for some people, even more. But, as all humans are different, we have different things that motivate us. One person could be motivated by money, and for another it could be recognition.

Many salespeople are financially motivated, and they say, 'I simply want to earn lots of money'. In my experience, the more specific the better, it becomes much more motivational. You would hardly go into the gym and say I'd like to become a beef cake.

I remember in 2005 when I decided it was time to propose. My first task was to enquire about an engagement ring and off with the mother-in-law I went. At £2000, I thought this was going to take me forever, as I was only able to put away around £20 a month. So, I set myself goals and broke it down specifically.

At that time I was selling software and had a very transparent commission structure. So, I gave myself six months to save for a ring, so I needed to save £333 a month to achieve my goal. This was £83.25 per week, and I worked out an average order value for commission of £45 per deal, so I required two extra deals a week to hit my goal.

My conversion rate at that time was 1 in 2.5 meetings, so I needed to attend a further five meetings per week. As I monitored and measured my figures very closely, I was aware that I needed to make 68 calls to get hold of 5 decision-makers a day and I converted 1 in 2 to a meeting. So, I needed to make an additional 28 calls a day to get hold of an additional 2 decision-makers, which would enable me to get that extra 1 meeting. By being this specific every day, I knew clearly what was required and I wouldn't leave the office until I had made my desired call rate.

I am pleased to say I achieved this goal in four months and she said 'yes'.

As a sales professional, establish what you are looking to achieve and break it into digestible chunks, no matter how big the goal seems. If your goals are tangible, such as a new car, I have seen many of my clients have a printout of their exact car, colour and model they desire placed in front of them on their desk. Their visual reminder every day keeps up their motivation and is a daily reminder of why they are working. So, when it's getting to 17:28 p.m. and normally they'll be thinking what are they having for dinner or who are they meeting at the pub, their mind can remain focused on their goal. It can drive them to make those extra calls that are needed to achieve their end result.

This concept can be applied to every area within your life. If you are looking to lose weight, you need to set a specific goal, within a specific time scale, and then work out what task you'll be doing to help you achieve this goal. The motivation comes when you stand on those scales and see that pin getting nearer and nearer to your desired weight. Remember, it's one step at a time, as Rome wasn't built in a day.

Your goals are something that will change as your life changes. When I had my first child, Harry, my goals changed dramatically. I am still a materialistic person; however, I felt the Porsche could wait, as his schooling was more of a priority. I would always suggest setting short (1 year), medium (1–3 years) and long-term goals (3–10 years).

'It's not the size of the dog in the fight; it's the size of the fight in the dog'.

There is a great book I would recommend called *The Secret* by Rhonda Byrne, where she explains the 'law of attraction'. If you think positive thoughts, you will attract positive things into your life, and the same applies for negative thoughts. It provides some wonderful ideas, such as creating boards of images of things you want and regularly looking at them. The book has many real-life examples of peoples' successes based on advice given by Rhonda Byrne.

Every salesperson you look at, who outperforms you, had to start the same as you, or behind you. They just learned sales principles and techniques. It's about having the drive and ambition to want to learn them. 'Every winner was once a beginner'.

Be positive. Don't let failure/rejection get to you. If you haven't achieved a sale, but you're sure you did everything right, then that is a job well done. Just approach the next customer with the same attitude.

If you've identified where you went wrong or could have done something better, make a mental note and make sure you don't make the same mistake again.

It's only rejection if you treat it as a rejection; ask yourself, 'What can I learn from this to do different next time?'

This reminded me of a time I was working with a client in Belfast called Henderson food service. They're a huge business, £650 million turnover and the largest employer in Belfast. They own 50% of the Spar franchises and all of the Vivo franchises in Ireland. I was helping about 35 of their BDMs, whose role was to manage accounts like cafes, restaurants, pubs, etc., and supply them with food and products. They had become 'order takers' and my brief was to help them cross-sell and upsell and become 'order makers'. After just two days training, the difference was sensational. The average order value had increased by 27%, and the teams were more motivated than ever before.

A few months later, I got a call from Kiera, their sales director. She phoned to thank me for the training and said the team is still smashing it and they keep referring back to techniques I taught them. I said it's my absolute pleasure. She said the other reason for the call is our parent company Country Range food group wants to train the salespeople across their 17 brands, and Henderson is just one of them. The board of directors has reached out to all the sales directors of all 17 brands and asked if anyone has any recommendations.

This is such a key part of sales. Reputation is what people say when you are NOT there.

Keira went on to say, of course I highly recommended you. She said, 'You will have to fly to Belfast and present to the 17 directors and you will be up against two other training companies, but between you and me, I'm quite influential with the board and my vote will go a long way'.

'Firstly, thank you so much for making me aware of the opportunity and secondly, for recommending me, it means a huge deal to me'. I asked what are the next steps?

Keira explained, the PA to the CEO of Country Range food group will reach out to me in the next couple of days and give me the necessary details.

I put the phone down and was ecstatic. In my head this was a done deal. Seventeen companies all with their own sales teams. This will be the biggest deal I ever do in my life.

I eagerly awaited the email from the PA, and it came a couple of days later. She emailed me dates and times of when I will be presenting and the names of all of the attendees. She gave me contact details of 1 of the

17 directors, called James, as he was providing the brief to the training companies. I called James immediately and booked a one-hour meeting with him to go through the brief the following week.

I started doing my research on all 16 directors, as I already knew Keira reasonably well. I was researching their businesses and getting an insight into their sales teams.

A week later, I had my call with James, and he was charming. We discussed the brief, and I asked him about the number of salespeople who will need training. I almost fell off my chair when he said 1200 people. He explained the board does not want a one-off training event; this will be an ongoing training program. I was trying really hard to act cool, calm and collected, even though I wanted to scream at the top of my voice; yet I restrained myself and acted as a consummate professional.

Now it was prep time. I spent several evenings practising my presentation, so I knew it inside out and back to front. I wanted to come across so well prepared that I was the only viable option for them. I practised it to my wife and to my kids, even Buddy, my gorgeous Poochon, watched it. When I say he watched it, he grabbed my PowerPoint clicker and hid it, which we still haven't found.

The day had arrived. I was nervous and excited; I knew I'd done my homework. I caught the flight to Belfast, and I started to design the Aston Martin Vantage I would buy when I won the contract. Midnight blue exterior with cream leather interior and navy stitching, I landed and jumped into a taxi and was at Country

Range's headquarters 30 minutes early. I waited patiently until I was asked to go in.

It was this lavish boardroom, with a long glass table and 19 directors sitting around it in silence, the 17 directors and 2 from Country Range. I recognised Keira and we both smiled and nodded. 'I've got this', I said to myself in my head.

I connected my laptop to the plasma, whilst someone poured me a glass of water. The butterflies kicked in and I was very aware of my heart beating and how dry my mouth seemed.

I began my presentation and after about 10 minutes one of the directors raised his hand. 'Yes', I said. 'How can we monitor the team's performance on a weekly basis?' he asked. I started talking about KPIs I would recommend and that I would suggest we outlined them before training was undertaken. He said, 'That's great, but can you show us an example'. I told him I didn't have an example to hand, but I could absolutely get one over to him. Another director then spoke up and said, 'This is the most important factor for us, as we must be able to review performance and need to get an idea of what that looks like'. I apologised and promised to get it over to them all.

My heart sank and that inner confidence suddenly dispersed. I continued through my presentation, and I became very aware that I had now lost some of their attention. A couple of them were checking their phones whilst I was speaking. I didn't have the courage to say anything and thought it would be a little confrontational to demand their attention. I finished my presentation and asked if anyone had any questions. Nothing. This was not a good sign.

I thanked them for their time, and they said they'd be in touch. I jumped in a taxi and headed back to the airport. I got on the plane and was home in under three hours. My wife asked how it went and I shared what happened. She reassuringly said you're brilliant at what you do, and your client personally recommended you on the results you helped her team achieve, so don't forget that. This was exactly the pep talk I needed.

The following day I got an email that read. 'Tony, we would like to thank you for taking the time to visit us and present to our organisation. It is with regret that. . .', and then everything after that was just a blur. I was devastated. All that effort I made in practising, the time I invested in prepping for it and the day out of the business to fly to Belfast and present; all for nothing. I was frustrated, angry and most of all disappointed. The time spent designing the Aston Martin was a total waste and was just a dream.

I feared telling my wife, as I was upset that I'd let her down. When I got home that evening I came straight out with it, 'They've gone with someone else'. She put her arms around me and said, 'There will be plenty more opportunities like that and now you've had practice at it'. She always had a great way of looking at things.

She asked what the feedback was, and I said, 'There wasn't any, just an email telling me they've chosen another training provider'. She insisted on me getting feedback, otherwise I would have taken nothing from this experience.

I replied to the email, thanking them for their prompt email and asked if I can set up a call to gain some feedback, and it was organised for the following week.

'Tony, we all thought you presented really well, but you didn't fulfil the brief'. James said the two most important parts of the brief were how do we measure the performance of the teams and how do we reinforce the learning. 'You didn't cover either of those points'.

It dawned on me; I spent so much time practising my presentation and not enough time digging deeper into the brief and ensuring the content I delivered was answering everyone's questions and concerns.

Of course, I was still disappointed; however, that lesson has been invaluable to me, and I have won more business on the back of it, than had I not learned it.

I think back to the experience with Mel and in this instance, I chose how to filter what occurred and that became my reality.

It was the great Nelson Mandela who said, 'You never lose, either you win or you learn'.

Reflect on Past Triumphs

Football clubs have trophy rooms to inspire performance, and salespeople should do the same with past sales (I guess it depends on what football club, but that is by the by).

If you experience a barren spell, find some records of your previous past deals, to remind yourself of your ability. This will restore or generate more confidence. You will only have improved since your last sale, so remember that if you could do it then, you can do it now!

I did some training with a client of mine in the waste management industry quite recently, and one of the sales guys, Chris, said to me that he had been out in the field all week doing appointments and door knocking and although he hadn't achieved any sales, he had an okay week. He walked into his depot on a Friday and his boss, Gary, asked him immediately how many deals he had done, to which he replied, 'None'.

'What kind of salesman are you, if you can't close a deal? And what have you been doing, watching Countdown? Why are you back in the office if you haven't done any business? Go out there and close'.

So, Chris asked me, 'How can I stay motivated and positive when I get that response every time I walk into the depot without a sale?'

My first bit of advice was, 'avoid Gary'. He is not a good leader, and he is only focusing on the numbers and not looking to develop or motivate you. I am afraid that motivation has to come from within.

I asked him, 'What did you achieve that week?' He replied, 'Weren't you listening? I got no sales at all, so nothing'.

'I guarantee you did achieve things; you are just closed off to it right now. So, let me ask you some questions', I said to him.

ME: How many new opportunities did you find that week that you didn't have at the beginning of the week?

CHRIS: Well, about eight, I guess, but surely if I didn't close them it's irrelevant?

ME: And out of those eight, how many decision-makers' names did you identify?

CHRIS: All of them; what's your point?

ME: Did you find out the situation within those eight companies?

CHRIS: Yeah, I found out the supplier they are with, the products they use and their contract date, but I didn't close any of them.

ME: What you are missing is, you are in a better position now than you were at the beginning of the week. You have identified eight new businesses with which you will be able to work with. If you stay in touch with them, there's a very strong possibility one of their suppliers will mess up and immediately you can get in. Equally, I would rather 10% of something than 100% of nothing, so it's worth positioning yourself as their back up supplier. You clearly qualified the prospect, who's to say in the near future their requirements don't change, and they may need something you offer that their suppliers cannot?

So, the key is *focus on what you did get*, as opposed to *focusing on what you didn't*. There will be days where you get hold of 40 companies that, for whatever reason, you cannot help. Rather than feeling depressed, understand that you had to call those 40 at some point, so at least you got them out of the way.

I recently worked with a sales guy from a client that I work with on a weekly basis, in the courier industry. He was fortunate enough to be involved in a £2 million tender to manage the entire logistics for one of the supermarket chains. He was up against the usual suspects like UPS, DHL, etc., and he had to compile a detailed tender document that he had to present on three occasions, to the senior management board and to some of the directors. He had to undertake many hours of research to complete this 85-page report, which was necessary to be involved in the tender. The entire process took seven weeks, then he got down to the last three and was not shortlisted for the final stage.

When he first read the email that thanked him for his efforts and explained that they will not be proceeding with his company, his face began to turn many different colours, from red to white, and then an odd, sickly colour. He had made the deadly schoolboy error in sales of spending the commission in his head before he won it, a real no-no for obvious reasons. He wanted to quit his job and said that he felt it was the biggest waste of time in the world and he had just thrown seven weeks of his life away for absolutely nothing.

I had to let him calm down for about three weeks, before explaining to him that he had learned some of the most valuable skills that he would be able to utilise in his sales career, like how to present to a board of directors and how to compile a huge tender document. He had learned more in the past seven weeks about logistics, than he had done in the past two years with the company. Yet in his anger and natural frustrated state, he was closed to all of these tools he had acquired, which would win him more business in the long run.

It's very easy for me to say from an outsider's perspective; however, having been on the losing side of many large opportunities, I take the view that I have lost it anyway, so I can either mope around and lose other opportunities or take the positives out of it and move on and find new opportunities. Which route would you rather choose to go down?

8

Building Rapport

'The ultimate measure of a man is not where he stands in moments of comfort and convenience, but where he stands in times of challenge and controversy'.

—Martin Luther King, Jr.

Kerry Johnson, the professional tennis player and author of *Selling with NLP* (neuro linguistic programming), defines building rapport as 'the bridge that helps the person you are communicating with find meaning and intent in the things you say'.

What Is Rapport?

It's about making people comfortable, gaining trust and putting people at ease. It is the start of building a relationship.

There are many strategies to build rapport. It is important to note that they will not all be suitable for everyone. The reason being we are all different.

I deliver many talks at sales conferences, often to a room of strangers. I notice that these strangers naturally begin gravitating towards people like themselves. This can be done without anyone actually speaking together; it's simply achieved through body language.

In the 1960s, there was a study carried out by two researchers, Dr Mehrabian and Dr Argyle, and they studied how do people communicate. In the circle provided in Figure 8.1, the three areas represent the following: the words we use, how we sound and body language.

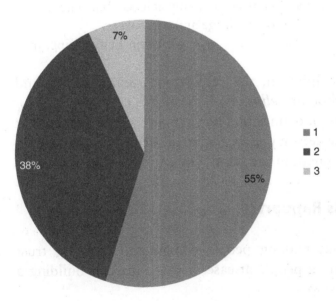

Figure 8.1

The words we use	%
How we say the words	%
Body language	%

Which percentage do you think applies to which of these three ways we communicate?

The words we use	7%
How we say the words	38%
Body language	55%

This study fascinated me. They found that the majority of how we communicate is nonverbal, without opening our mouths. I refused to take this at face value and I looked into other research. The findings always came back to the same results.

I think about my personal life. I love my wife Shana to bits; however, she has this really annoying habit; she makes lunch arrangements on the weekend with our kids' school friends' parents. I don't mean to be rude; however, I am a busy guy and I cannot be bothered making small talk with randoms on my weekend.

A few weeks ago, Shana said, 'Ethan's mum and dad have invited us over for Sunday lunch this weekend. 'Cosmic', I said. I turned to Shana and said, 'We are not going. I don't know how many more times we must have the same row, but you can go on, you can cancel it, but we are not going'.

And then we went. On the way to the house, Shana was driving, kids were sitting at the back of the car and we were not talking. We pulled up onto their drive, I got out the car and slammed the door, so Shana knew I was still pissed off. I approached the door, rang the doorbell and seconds later a random came to the door. I stuck my hand out and said, 'Hi, I'm Harry's dad'. He reached his hand out and grabbed mine but had that limp wet handshake, barely gripping mine.

I hated him. I took a glance back at my wife and gave her that death stare that said, 'I really hate you right now more than ever before'. She looked back at me and gave me the stare that said, 'I also hate you and nothing you can do about it'.

I turned back and walked into the limp-hand man's house. The food was nice, but it was a painful experience. Fortunately for me, Shana also found it uncomfortable and promised me we will never have to see them for lunch again. And to date, we haven't.

I have changed their names; in case they happen to read this book.

The point of the story is that I made a judgement within two seconds of meeting Ethan's dad. We are taught at school that don't judge a book by its cover, but that is not real life.

One of the first clients I ever delivered training to was an estate agent in Clapham in 2008. They were an independent estate agent and had a few branches spread across Clapham. I recall a story the director told me, when I started working with them. He said, 'A gentleman walked into one of their branches and walked up to the lady on the front desk and she looked him up and down'. He said to her, 'I am looking to buy a couple of properties for my daughters and was wondering if anyone is available to show me any?' The lady replied, 'I am sorry, but everyone is busy on appointments right now.' The gentleman was taken aback and said, 'Fine, don't worry about it in that case' and he left.

Eight weeks later, the same guy walked into the same branch and up to the same lady behind the front desk and said, 'I was in here a couple of months ago and I have never done this before, but do you know who I am?' The lady looked blankly at him and said 'I am really sorry, but no I don't'. He said, 'I am Sir Bob Geldof. And I really do not like how you treated me when I was last here. I bought two properties for Trixie and Peaches and spent over £11 million and maybe you should think about that, next time you look down at someone like me'.

As you can imagine, the director fired this lady on the same day that incident occurred. Interestingly, I was speaking at a property conference, in the South of France, for Beaux Villages. I shared this story, and once I finished my talk, I went over to grab a coffee. As I was pouring the milk in my cup, a lady approached me and said, 'You are not going to believe this but, when you told us this story about Bob Geldof, I texted my uncle, as he has run a boutique estate agency in Clapham for 28 years. Bob Geldof is his client.'

What a small world right. This is a great lesson – everyone you know knows someone you don't.

Going back to the study on communication, when you are communicating over the phone, you remove body language and are left with sound and words (Figure 8.2).

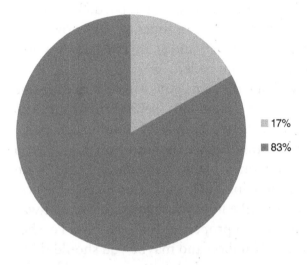

Figure 8.2

The words we use	%
How we say the words	%

Which percentage do you think applies to which of these two ways we communicate?

Words	17%
Sound	83%

So, here the words play a more significant role; however, how you sound is the vast majority of how we communicate over the phone. We have all heard the saying, 'It's not what you say, it's how you say it'.

I touched on this earlier in the chapter on preparation; the top sales professionals sound great on every call. The two strategies they use are the lesson and the whale, as they know how important it is to be on your A-Game on every single call.

A few years ago, I was conducting some telephone coaching to a client of mine, who specialises in selling UK and overseas property as an investment. There was a relatively new sales guy who was pitching a new investor on the phone and I was standing behind him, thinking how well he was doing. He exuded confidence, he was standing up and speaking at quite a high volume and at a fast pace. I then dialled into the call and heard the investor speaking for the first time. If I had to guess, I would have said the lady was approximately 70 years of age, with a very well-spoken voice and gentle tone. She spoke very slowly and pronounced her words very clearly. The sales guy clearly did not pick up on any of this, and treated everyone he spoke to in the same way. This is what you describe as a mismatch. So, how could he have dramatically improved the rapport?

In NLP, which I will discuss in greater depth in a later chapter, they state that to build rapport, you need to match or mirror; mirror being the reflection.

This is where the fun part comes in, as you get an opportunity to be an actor. The key is to be sincere, as people can sense insincerity quickly. It's like when you walk into a retail outlet in America and have the worst cold and feel like crap and the assistant says, 'Hi there, how are you today?', and you reply, 'I have the worst cold ever and feel like death'. They reply with that massive cheesy grin and say, 'Fantastic, well, have a wonderful day!'

So over the phone, how do we match people? These are the key things to listen out for and match:

Pace – The speed at which someone talks.
Pitch – How high or how low someone's voice is.
Timbre – The resonance of someone's voice.
Word inflections – The different ways to pronounce the same word. Although, please note, do not match a person's accent, this is called being racist.

On the phone, pay attention to the different voice aspects of people. When you have picked up something, try and match it.

If the person speaks quietly, you need to lower your volume and speak quietly. If the person speaks slowly, you need to slow your pace and speak slowly. If they have a particular tone of voice, you need to match this tone carefully. Imagine speaking to an 80-year-old woman over the phone and then to a 25-year-old man; I am sure you'll agree the pace, tone, timbre and volume will all be extremely different.

There is one other area that you need to match and this could win or lose you a deal.

One of the first whales I landed was with a list broking company that sells consumer data. They had around 80 salespeople and I was meeting Graham, who was the head of sales.

In the meeting, I asked Graham, 'If you were to move forward with us, what are your key objectives for the sales training?' He said, 'It's crucial that we separate the wheat from the chaff'. I maintained the look of understanding and professionalism plastered across my face, despite not understanding the term. I noted it down along with his other seven key objectives, and continued the meeting.

I found out afterwards, 'separate the wheat from the chaff' is a farmer's term, but in sales it means 'get rid of the salespeople that simply do not want to learn or develop, and have given up'. So, when I came to do my proposal three days later, I had my eight objectives bullet-pointed on the first page and clearly the top line read 'Separate the wheat from the chaff'.

I am not saying that's the reason I won the deal; however, when Graham looked at my proposal against the four other training companies, he probably would have thought, 'Tony thinks just like me', and therefore was the best person to deliver training to his team.

What Did I Match?

His language. It's imperative that you use their exact words and do not use an alternative that you prefer, as it will not resonate with them. So, if you are a negotiator showing an applicant a property and they say, 'I am looking for something luxurious with lots of character', then those two keywords must be used later when you take them around the property.

Using Keywords

Those who have interviewed Bill Gates, the chairman of Microsoft, remark on how he peppers his speech with technical terms related to programming, for example, bandwidth, random, hardcore, etc. Using them regularly shows how important that 'techie' side of him still is. Therefore, those who use such words back to him are the ones who have an edge in getting hired. If you can meaningfully use the jargon in your presentation or on a meeting back to a prospect, do it, it's a great rapport builder.

A life insurance broker had a meeting with a lady who wanted advice on financial planning. He heard her say that she wanted 'protection, with an increase in income as an investment'. He was used to saying, 'security with high protection'. He adapted by saying, 'I understand that you want protection with an increase in income. Here's how this product will help you. . .'.

I would recommend keeping a note of words and phrases your prospect uses, and use those back to them, when you sum up the meeting or later in your proposal.

Along with matching people over the phone, it's also paramount to match them face to face. I recall a meeting I had with one of my biggest clients. He is the MD of a company who turns over approximately £75 million and is extremely direct and brash. He is a beaming red in Carl Jung's behaviour matrix (to be shared shortly), and he smells small talk a mile off and doesn't tolerate it. When I speak to him, I try and communicate in bullet points, with clear precise statements that get across what's in it for him.

His body language is very different to other clients of mine, and my job is to adapt accordingly. He always gets up very close to me and I call that, 'a space invader'. This makes me very uncomfortable, but it's not about me.

The second thing he does is he uses many hand gestures when explaining an idea or trying to get his point across, so I make a point when summarising a situation or getting across my point to use many hand gestures, which, on a subconscious level, will make my client comfortable.

The third and final thing my client does is he plays with an object when sitting down at his desk. He either taps a pen or fiddles with a paper clip. I use the technique of cross-matching where I may tap my foot as he taps his pen, which will maintain rapport with my client.

Have you ever seen a person yawn and then you find yourself yawning? I always used to think to myself, *I am not tired, so why am I yawning, just because I saw someone else do it?* In NLP, they call this 'instantaneous rapport', which means you have created an immediate rapport with a stranger on a subconscious level.

You can test this concept in your next meeting. Start to tap your pen against the table very discreetly throughout the meeting. I guarantee, by the end, the majority of people in that room will be tapping their pen or an object against the desk, or cross-matching you without even giving it a second thought. Once you have mastered influencing people around you, take this new-formed skill into your sales meetings or presentations and see what impact it has.

We know 'matching' is one way to build rapport, so what are the other ways?

The Two Golden Rules of Rapport

There are two well-known sayings in sales, which I would like to discuss.

The first is, 'Treat people how. . .'.

How do you believe this will end?

Treat people how you would like to be treated. You are more than likely familiar with this, and my late dad mentioned this many times to me growing up.

However, he was wrong. There was one word that needs to change. Any idea?

Treat people how THEY would like to be treated. It is not about you, it's all about them. How can you treat everyone how you want to be treated, as you are different to them.

In 2011, I won a large kitchen retailer client. At that time, they had around 80 stores and now have over 200. Once I won the contract, the founder, Malcolm, asked me to go down the corridor and introduce myself to the

MD, a gentleman by the name Armando, as he will become my main point of contact.

I walked down the corridor, saw Armando's name on the door and knocked until I was invited in.

ARMANDO: Come in.

ME: Hi there, you must be Armando?

ARMANDO: I am indeed.

ME: My name is Tony Morris, and my team and I will be delivering all the sales training to all your sales reps around the country. Malcolm just asked me to come and introduce myself to you.

ARMANDO: Well, you've done that now.

ME: Okay then.

As I walked back out his office, I thought to myself, what's his problem?

A few weeks later, after my team and I had delivered training to a few of the stores, I had a question I needed to ask Armando. I called his PA, who put me straight through.

ARMANDO: Armando speaking.

ME: Hi Armando, it's Tony Morris speaking, how are you?

ARMANDO: I am good, thank you.

ME: Good stuff. I just wanted to ask about the team at the Milton Keynes office. How did you want to split the team up for training?

ARMANDO: Have you met Laura, the Milton Keynes store manager?

ME: I will be meeting her next Wednesday.

ARMANDO: Call her on 07915..., and ask her the question.

ME: Okay, thanks.

What is that guy's beef? I thought to myself. He absolutely hates me. I could not work out what I did to him, and it started to really bother me.

A couple of weeks later, I observed Armando running a meeting with 35 of the store managers. I was pleased to see he acted as direct and blunt with all of them as he did with me. It made me realise, it wasn't me, it was him; this is just how he is.

About a month later, I had to make a call to Armando again. Although the thought of it filled my stomach with dread, I thought to myself, I now know it's not me, and don't take it personally. And if he is direct, then I'll be direct and play him at his own game.

ARMANDO: Armando speaking.

ME: Armando, Tony Morris. Reason for my call is, I feel a few of the store managers could benefit from sales management training and one of my experts, John, can really help them. Can I organise it?

ARMANDO: Yes, get it arranged.

ME: Good stuff.

And it then hit me. Armando wasn't being rude, he was being red (to be discussed shortly). In his world, he is not rude at all. He has absolutely no idea the impact he has on others, and, more importantly, doesn't really care. If people didn't like his approach, that was their problem, not his. This is certainly not a lesson for leadership, but this is a lesson for understanding behaviours.

The other golden rule of rapport is, 'people buy from. . .'.

How does this end? 'People buy from people'. This I agree with, as people buy with emotion and then logic comes in to justify their buying decision.

Last weekend, I was out for clothes shopping with the kids. I went past a men's clothes shop, and there was the most incredible knitted jumper on a mannequin. I thought to myself, I would look like Brad Pitt in that jumper. I managed to persuade the kids to come in with me by saying I'd get them both chocolate straight after this. We never stop selling.

I was looking around the shop to find this jumper and there was only one on the shelf, but it was a large one. I asked the shop assistant if they have it in a medium and he said, 'they don't have'. Then he said, 'I think the one on the mannequin is a medium one, let me have a quick look'. It was a medium one. I eagerly took it from him and went straight to the changing room like an eager beaver, with the kids dragging behind me. I tried it on and then stepped outside the changing room to see my reflection in the floor to ceiling mirror. I did the different poses you do in front of the mirror to take in all the different angles. I thought to myself, Brad Pitt would not look as good as I look in this jumper. I looked at my kids for approval and they both nodded and said it really suited me. I then took it off to see the price tag. My heart sank when I read £949. I loved it, but I didn't love it that much. I handed it back to the shop assistant and walked out the shop to get the kids chocolate, and myself some, to overcome my misery.

The emotion is what got me into the shop, the logic is what prevented me from buying it.

However, apart from taking the jumper off the mannequin, the shop assistant did absolutely nothing to try and persuade me otherwise. I'm not saying he could have told me around to spend £949, but if you don't ask the question, then the answer will always be a no.

Although the golden rule is 'people buy from people'. I believe two four-letter words are missing here.

People buy from people _____

_____

Like Them

People buy from people like them. What they mean by this is people feel most comfortable when dealing with people like themselves, when they find things in common, and they have the same outlook.

Therefore, in addition to matching people, another great way to build rapport is to imagine every person you meet has a board above their head that reads, 'It's all about me'. We know people love to talk about themselves, so let them. The Pareto's law of 80/20 kicks in again – it should be 80% them talking about themselves.

One of the greatest pieces of advice I ever heard when it came to rapport was this – you don't need to be interesting, be interested. Imagine you go on a blind date. You are both a little nervous and then you meet at a restaurant. You take a seat at the table and your blind date says to you, 'Tell me about yourself'. You then start telling them about where you grew up, your past relationships, and after five minutes, they are losing the will for YOU to live. They will just be thinking what excuse I can use to leave this table run. The quicker you make it about them, the better.

I had a guest on my podcast, *Confessions of a Serial Seller*. I spent the first 45 seconds introducing my guest and then asked the question, 'How did you get into the world of selling?' I am not exaggerating when I say, 39 minutes later he was still talking. I then said, 'Really great hearing your story and what is the best way for my listeners to connect with you?' This was my way of allowing him to plug his books or anything else he wanted to direct my listeners too. About six minutes later, I thanked him for joining me and wished him well. I turned the record button off and thanked him once again. He said to me, 'Tony that was such a good chat'. I wish I were making this up. He was probably oblivious that he had just spoken at me for nearly 45 minutes. If you let someone talk, and you listen and you ask a couple of questions to demonstrate you're interested, then you win.

9
Who Is Your Ideal Client?

'It's hard to beat a person who never gives up'.
—Babe Ruth

Before we discuss your ideal client, I want you to think about these two words: prospect and suspect.

A prospect is a business or an individual you can help. It's a business or an individual that is experiencing problems that you have solved in the past, or have the ability to solve. It's a business or an individual that is right for you or your business. This can be broken down into several criteria, such as:

- Number of employees.
- Turnover.
- Industry type.
- Markets they operate in.

- Growth plans.
- Who they relate to.
- Sister companies.

A suspect is a business or an individual that does not fit your criteria. You need to disqualify a suspect, so your time is invested wisely.

I ask many salespeople, 'Who is your ideal customer?', and they normally respond by saying 'Anyone our products and services suit, literally anybody'. The immediate challenge I see with this is that it makes it very difficult for you to target your ideal customer.

When I sold address management software at the beginning of my sales career, I was given a large geographical area to target and told to go out and sell. With minimal sales experience, I invested in myself and attended a two-day sales workshop that provided many useful ideas and techniques that I use to this day. One that sticks out for me the most is to grade your clients and your prospects. The trainer explained that if you are responsible for generating new business, you should look back at your company's client base and grade them into four levels.

Grade A are your ideal clients and you have to decide what they mean to you. For example, they might pay the most, have a shorter sales cycle, easier to covert, you enjoy working with them the most, bigger opportunity to cross-sell other products/services in your portfolio, makes a good strategic alliance (explained later on in the book).

Grade B are your bread-and-butter clients. These are the ones your company tends to do most business with and have been your longest-serving clients.

Grade C are your one-off clients. They are ones that are unlikely to buy again from you, and you have minimal opportunity to cross-sell your other products/ services too. In my world, these are clients that book me to speak at a conference, yet they are very unlikely to book me for sales training, for a number of reasons.

Grade D are your dead clients. These are ones you want to avoid like the plague. They are ones that spend the least and probably create most of your problems. You have some in mind as you're reading this. One of the clients I took on at the early start of my sales training company paid me the least and was by far the most demanding. They took up so much of my time, and for very little reward. It was only until my company grew, that I was able to move away from them and invest my time more wisely, targeting the right type of client for my business.

Once you've graded your clients, it's time to look for trends. As an example, going back to when I sold software, I noticed that 70% of the Grade A clients were large call centres and banks. So, I was confused why the majority of the sales team were calling everybody and anybody, then I realised that I was the only one who had graded the clients. When I asked the sales team, who uses our software they replied, 'everybody'. So, when they invested the same amount of time and energy to win a Grade C client who spent £3500, I was spending my time on the right company and winning a £200,000 deal, with very little extra effort. It didn't take them long to catch on to what I was doing and start copying this simple, yet effective formula. Once I established who our Grade A clients were, I then began to build my hit list.

Then you can grade a level deeper. Once I got this, my mindset changed again. This grading is when you are thinking about growth and expansion for your business, and it complements the Grade A to D tiers.

The 8/10, 9/10 and 10/10 clients are described as your dream clients, ultimately a Grade A client. These can be defined by different metrics to Grade As that I just discussed. These can be:

- Growth potential for the client.
- Their involvement with other sister companies.
- To use as a credibility piece to win other clients like them.

The more you focus on these, the more they turn up. It's the same concept that I discuss in the NLP chapter; when you buy a white car and suddenly, loads of white cars turn up. They were always there, but you just were not focused on them. So, once you start winning more 8/10 to 10/10, more will show up and you'll find it much more comfortable turning away the 1/10 to 6/10, which you may have taken in the past, due to desperation to hit your targets and make your numbers.

A 1/10 to 6/10 are ones that you want to avoid. These can be defined in several ways, and here are a few points to illustrate them:

- Always try and push you on your prices.
- Hard work to deal with.
- They demand long payment terms and always pay late.
- Want lots done and not prepared to pay for it.

The 7/10 clients become your biggest problem. They could become an 8/10 client, equally they could be draining and become a 6/10 client. On the outset, they seem attractive, and you'll be tempted to work with them. However, tread carefully, as if they start to become a 6/10, they can start to drain your time and energy.

The reason you must be selective with who you choose to work with is they become a magnet. Therefore, if you work with many 4/10s, they will naturally magnetise more 4/10 clients to you. Partly because you'll do a great job and they will refer you to their connections, which are very likely to be people or businesses like theirs. This is not always the case; however, you find people are often connected with people like themselves; they hang around in the same group of networks. There is no coincidence that many successful entrepreneurs and business owners are connected to many other successful entrepreneurs and business owners.

Once you have understood your Grade As and 8/10 to 10/10, now you can start targeting more effectively.

Building Your Hit List

Your hit list is a list of your ideal clients. This can only be created once you have graded and numbered all of your clients. So, once I knew my Grade As and 10/10s, I started to make a list of all their competition. The great part about this is once you have achieved success with one company in an industry, it becomes your success story. You can use this success story in all your prospecting calls to their competitors. And I will go into much greater detail later in the book.

What I've discussed is about direct clients; however, I recommend you profile companies that could be a great strategic alliance for your business. The definition of this is 'a company that has the same target market as you and offers a different product or service that ideally compliments your offering'. When thinking about strategic alliances for Tony Morris International, my sales training company, my thought process was as follows.

Strategic Alliances

Who is my ideal target audience? This splits into two; the decision-maker(s) who signs off on the training, which are sales directors and managing directors, and the salespeople who attend our training. Which companies have the exact same target audience?

Sales recruitment firms, list brokers (companies who provide leads), outsourced telemarketing companies, etc.

are the ones that I identified. I did research which companies are well respected in these fields and made contact to create an alliance. The key message I had to communicate to the MDs of these companies was 'what's in it for them?' Like everything in sales, if this isn't crystal clear in the initial 15 to 20 seconds, then it will be extremely challenging to engage someone.

When it comes to strategic alliances, you need to consider upfront a few options for the commercial agreement. As an example, it could be a % of the deal you're happy to give away to the company you collaborate with. It could be a case of no money is passed and you just look to help one another. In my experience, the more motivated you are to make introductions, the more likely they are to make them.

The company may have the same target audience, in terms of the industry, although they may have a different decision-maker to you. A good friend of mine runs a company that supplies products to over 2000 hotel companies, that is, toiletries, dressing gowns, slippers, etc. Their decision-makers are head of purchasing or head of housekeeping. My decision-maker in the hotel industry is the director of sales. However, we were both able to buy a database of hotel groups and request the different decision-makers outlined earlier and split the costs of the database. In addition, we have joined up at hotel exhibitions and got a good size exhibition stand and both advertised our different offering.

Ideally, you want a strategic alliance that has exactly the same decision-makers as you. In addition to the financial gain, more importantly, you must think about the benefit to your client base. As an example, I have collaborated with the leading CRM system for estate agents. Their solution helps estate agents record data on their prospects and clients, as well as managing their pipeline and lots more. My training solution helps estate agents turn those prospects into clients. Therefore, it adds huge value when their CRM company says to their client, 'in addition to helping you manage the data you are recording, we have collaborated with the leading sales training company in the property industry, who have successfully helped our clients convert their prospects into clients (notice the language I used: successfully helped our clients, as opposed to worked with; and then they delivered the result of converting their prospects into clients).

This benefit works both ways. I was able to say to my estate agents clients, 'Once I have helped you win more business, I have collaborated with the leading CRM company, who has successfully helped my clients manage their client base more effectively to ensure they are maximising every opportunity and not leaving any money on the table'.

In sales, you cannot work with everyone. Firstly, you don't have the time and secondly many companies are not the right fit for your business. One of my old mentors, Nigel Risner, taught me the three 'F' rule, when it came to deciding if you want to work with a client. This stood for 'fit, fee, flee'. This is what Nigel explained.

How to Be Seen as the Expert in Their Field

When you target a specific industry and a company within that industry, it's important to come across as an expert in their field. This builds credibility and enables them to trust and value your opinion. This sounds so obvious; however, I cannot tell you how many hundreds of salespeople I've met that were targeting a company and couldn't tell me anything about the market. There are a few ways to become an expert in an industry, and here are some of those ways.

Use Their Language

Each industry will have its own language. I recommend cresting a glossary for each industry you serve. As an example, for estate agents, they don't call it meetings; they call it viewings or valuations. For recruitment, they don't call their sales team, salespeople, they call them recruitment consultants. It is imperative that you use the language of your prospect to ensure they don't underestimate what you're talking about and to demonstrate you understand their industry.

Google Alerts

For those who are unaware of this genius tool, let me explain. As the name suggests, you create a Google alert account and type in the words and companies that you wish Google to alert you about. I have set up an alert for all of my clients of my sales training company. Recently, I received an email alert that one of my estate agency clients was opening another branch. I sent them a hand-written card and a plant for their new branch, wishing them congratulations. Obviously, this was followed up with a phone call a week later, to see how the opening went. On the back of that conversation, they booked some training for the new negotiators that they had recruited. I'm not just a nice guy, I'm a sales professional!

So, as well as giving you a reason to call all of your clients and show that you know what's going on in their world, it can be used for your prospects as well. Once you have created a hit list, you can enter all of their company names in your Google alerts account, to ensure you're aware of exactly what's happening with them. It allows you to keep your finger on the pulse with no effort required. Therefore, when you call the prospects, you are able to share some insights of what is happening in their industry to demonstrate you know what is happening in their world.

One Google alert generated my company around £85,000 and my one becomes three. One morning, I received a Google alert that the director of sales for MacDonalds hotel, Gill, was leaving. I called Gill that day to make sure she was okay, and she asked how I knew about it the news. I explained that I always keep my finger on the pulse with my clients. Again, this builds trust, as you are demonstrating that you genuinely care about your clients. In that conversation, Gill explained she left, as she was joining a new hotel group called

LGH Hotels. Within four weeks of starting, Gill booked me to speak at their sales kick-off conference. On the back of the conference, she booked me for a 12-month training program. This was going really well until COVID began and the training was put on hold. Although frustrating, I was always taught, only focus on things IN YOUR control.

I asked Gill who replaced her at MacDonalds, and it was a gentleman called Richard. Rather than me cold call Richard, I asked Gill to do an email introduction, as this is always a better way in. Within two weeks, Richard and I had met, and he booked me to deliver training for his team, some of whom I had trained before.

Then the final opportunity arose. Where did Richard leave to join MacDonalds? I did ask, however, it was a huge global hotel group that had an internal training academy, so was a non-starter.

It is so important to stay in touch with your clients and follow their career. LinkedIn has made this so easy for salespeople; only if you have connected with all your clients on LinkedIn.

Trade Publications

In addition to Google alerts, I would recommend you read the magazines your clients read. Let me give an example of the value of this. As I train many estate agents, I subscribe to a lot of the property magazines such as PIE (Property Industry Eye), as it's imperative that my clients know I'm an expert in their field and I'm aware of what's going on in their market. I was reading an article about a year ago, about Prospect estate agency, which was acknowledged for their signage on their branches. I happened to be recommended to Prospect, three weeks later and I mentioned to the MD about what a great article it was and I could see from his expression he was impressed I had read the article, especially as I'm not an agent. I don't know if that's why I won the deal; however, it didn't hurt.

Exhibitions

There are many industry exhibitions. It is worth attending for a couple of reasons. Firstly, it's a great prospecting opportunity. I remember going to my first property investment exhibition a year after setting my training company up, back in 2007. I saw a stand called EMP Advisers. There were quite a few people on the stand, which caught my attention. I approached a guy on the stand, and he looked at me and said, 'Can I help you?' This a terrible question to try and engage a prospect. Why? Because it allows the prospect to politely say, 'No, thank you'. Remember, if you do not want to hear a no, do not ask a question that could get a no. A better question would have been, 'What brings you here today?' Some people will say, 'I got here by car', but you cannot win them all.

So, I said to the guy, 'You might be able to help me, what is it you do?' I asked. He then opened up his mouth and spoke at me for what felt like an hour. I call this 'sales vomit' and no one likes to be vomited on. Remember Pareto's law, the 80/20 rule. It would have been better to reply, 'We help people make their money work better for them, through property investments. What do you do?'

After his sales vomiting, I said, 'That sounds interesting. And I can tell you're in sales (although clearly not very good at it, I thought to myself), who can I speak to that would be responsible for developing the sales team?' He introduced to me Jamal, who was the founder of EMP Advisers.

That sales guy spent what felt like an hour, wasting his time and energy on me, where he could have invested that time speaking to someone who might buy his product/service. An important element of sales is know who are your prospects and who are your suspects. Your prospects are people you can potentially work with and are worth investing your time in. Suspects are people that will waste your time and you want to give those people as little of your time as possible.

What Do You Do?

Jamal said to me, 'So I understand you want to talk to me. What is it that you do?'

This is a really important question and one you will hear a lot, especially at networking events. When someone says, 'What do you do?', what are they really asking you? They are asking, 'How can you help me?'

When I am networking, and I ask people, 'What do you do?' These are the common responses I get back:

'I am an accountant'.
'I am a project manager'.
'I am an IFA (independent financial adviser)'.

This is NOT what you do, this is what YOU ARE. I am an accountant, a project manager, an IFA.

So, next time someone asks you, 'What do you do?' You need to be able to answer it in two ways:

Whom do you help?
How do you help them?

So, I replied to Jamal, 'I have helped many properties investment companies double their sales figures, without spending an extra penny on marketing'. And then I closed my mouth and I watched him digest that information.

I could have said, 'I am a sales trainer. I run a sales training company. I have been in sales for eight years'. However, all he would have heard was, 'Bore, bore, bore, bore'. Instead, I did not tell him any of that, I simply told him whom I help and how I help them. He replied, 'How do you help them double their sales figures?' So, what has happened here? He is curious and I now have his attention. To which I replied, 'I can see your busy exhibiting today, let's set up a meeting at a time that suits us both and I can explain how I have achieved that in great detail'. I then got my mobile phone out and gave him a couple of dates and times that suited me. I booked a time and took his email and mobile phone number, my goal was achieved.

Facebook Groups

The final way to become an expert in your client's field is to hang around online, where they hang around. There will be many Facebook groups that your clients and prospects will be members of. If they are members, and you have helped them, it's more than likely there will be other companies like them that you can help too. One important tip here is do not turn up and pitch. This is seen as commission breath and people do not like the smell of it. Instead, share ideas, give value, share links to articles or things that would benefit the members of the group. This way, you are seen as someone who is there to help, not as a pushy salesperson that is desperate for business.

10
Getting Past the Gatekeepers

'If you want to conquer fear, don't sit home and think about it. Go out and get busy'.

—Dale Carnegie

If you have seen the film 'Boiler Room', you would have learned that the 'gatekeeper' is the person on reception whose role entails stopping cold callers getting through.

Most salespeople are under the impression they must speak to them in a certain way, normally with no respect, and that will get past them. This could not be further from the truth. The first thing to do is to treat them like a human being, and ask for their help. They'll normally, not always, respond positively. Here is an example of this:

GATEKEEPER: Good morning.

SALESMAN: Good morning, my name is Tony Morris from the TMI, who am I speaking with please?

GATEKEEPER: Michelle.

SALESMAN: Hi Michelle, as I said my name is Tony and I really hope you can help. I train and develop sales teams, and the person I normally speak to in a business of your size is the head of learning and development. Who do you recommend would be the best person to speak to about that, Michelle?

I cannot guarantee a result, as it depends on certain factors – the person, how busy they are and what they have been told to say by their company (although the more charming you can be, the more likely they are to bend the rules slightly). Remember to record Michelle's name in your CRM system or whatever you use to record information, so when you call back and she answers you can remember to say, 'Good afternoon, Michelle, and how's your day going today?' This little bit of rapport you have built has put you one step ahead of your competition, and that step may be all you need to be given a contact name.

One very common objection a gatekeeper may give you is called a 'no name policy' – if you haven't got the contact's name, they can't put you through. This is where a little creative selling comes into play.

If you are uncomfortable in using any of the following techniques and white lies, then do not use them. All I can tell you is that they have worked with me and helped me to get through to the decision-maker and demonstrate the value we can bring to the table, resulting in a great deal of business and, therefore, commission. However, sales is all about being comfortable and having confidence. If you are not confident, it will be very apparent, and then you will fail.

Please see the following text for the 'no name' techniques that have put my clients and me in front of decision-makers, and generated new business:

1. Make up a name.

ME: Good morning, can I speak to Mike Beard please?
MICHELLE: We don't have a Mike Beard here.
ME: I have him down as the sales director, who has taken over his position? (Michelle says it's actually John Smith.)

Calling a couple of days later and chatting with Michelle can easily get you John Smith's number.

ME: Hi there, I hope you can help. I have been calling John Smith's mobile number and it goes through to a female voicemail message, so I assume I have written it down wrong. Can you please confirm the number I have been given, please?

Read out your own mobile number if they ask you to repeat it. About 30% of the time the gatekeeper says, 'You have completely the wrong number, the one you need is X'.

It gives immense satisfaction when the gatekeeper would not initially give you the decision-maker's name, and you now have their name and mobile number. Here's another way:

ME: Hi, it's Tony Morris here from TMI and I am just updating my records. Is Mike Beard still the sales director? If not, who's taken over his role?

2. Go on their website.

There will usually be a name mentioned somewhere in the 'Meet the Team' section or in the news pages. It might not be the contact you are after, but you can use that name when you call back. 'Good morning, perhaps I have spoken to a wrong person in the past who was unable to recommend the right person to talk. Who would you suggest deals with training and development in your sales team?'

3. Be aware of the times to call.

If you do have the directors' names, but the gatekeeper doesn't put you through, call during times the gatekeeper is unlikely to be there – before 08:45 a.m./12:15–13:45 p.m./after 17:30 p.m.

4. Use LinkedIn to find a name.

This is the easiest way to find a name and see who they're connected with. In addition, below their name, you can see written 'people have also viewed these connections', which could be the decision-maker you actually need.

5. Make a joke of the 'no name' response.

This must be done with charm and wit or you will get called a variety of rude names like I have been in the past.

GATEKEEPER: I'm afraid it's a 'no name' policy.
ME: I understand that, and sorry, who am I speaking with?
GATEKEEPER: Michelle.
ME: I think you may have just broken your policy, Michelle.

I sometimes get, 'Good one, $%£$%$%', and the lovely sound of a dead phone line. Other times, you'll get a laugh and say, 'Michelle, please help. I'm not looking for anything confidential and I promise to not mention your name when I speak to the right person'.

6. Gatekeepers are trained to ask, 'Are they expecting your call?' Your response must always be 'I'm returning their call'. And when the person comes on the phone and question you, 'You said I was returning you call?' You should say, 'Absolutely, do you not remember?' When they say 'no', say, 'I won't take offence, I'm not that memorable. Look, to refresh your memory. . .'. and then go into your pitch.

Always ask for your contact by their first name, as this gives the impression you know them personally.

7. With software such as Cognism, Lusha, Apollo.io, RocketReach, etc., you should never have an issue on getting someone's name. It's worth doing the research, as you can waste so much time not getting through, which is the time that should be spent having good conversations, where you are qualifying them in or disqualifying them out.

Voice Mails

Now there have been many debates in sales whether to leave voice mails, and if so, what do you say? Here's what I say:

'Hi Steve, its Tony. Give us a bell back on. . . . Thanks'.

I get approximately 60% of people call me back from a cold call, and my voice mail is very straightforward and I have labelled it 'the ambiguous "voice mail"'.

Do not state your surname, your company name or the reason for your call. By using the informal language, the prospect falls into the trap and returns your call from curiosity alone. You may be thinking, *I wouldn't return that voice mail*, and you may be right, but then you would fall into that 40%. If you don't try, you'll never know.

When they do call you back, this is how the conversation should go:

ME: Tony speaking.

PROSPECT: Yes, hi Tony. It's NAME here, I got a voice mail to call you.

ME: Thanks for returning my call. Are you familiar with us?

PROSPECT: No, never heard of you.

ME: That's okay. I'm sure you'll recognise the clients we have helped.

And then go into your pitch. Remember, talk to them about how you have helped your clients and the results you helped them achieve. The key of a voice mail is to get them to call you back and then it's your job to turn that into an opportunity.

Once I leave a voice email, I make sure I have sent them email, asking when is a convenient time for us to speak. If I have their mobile number, I will also send them a text. I call this 'VET' every call – voice mail, email and text. You have tripled the probability of them returning your call.

11
Smart Calling

'Don't focus on how to spend less money, focus on how to make more money'.

—Richard Denny

What is the difference between smart calling and cold calling?

As the name suggests, smart calling involves doing a little bit of research before the call. I would recommend not more than three minutes, as you may end up with a voicemail. I learned this term and some wonderful ideas and techniques from a fantastic US sales guru, Art Sobczak, in his incredible book, *Smart Calling*.

Cold calling is where you literally are going in cold, with no contact name, no idea about the company or industry you are calling, no angle as to how you can help or add value to the business, etc. Many sales gurus claim cold calling does not work anymore, as buyers have wised up to them. To some extent, I agree, but smart calling does work.

When preparing to make a smart call, there are certain steps I always think about:

Step 1: What does the company I am about to call actually do?

Once I know this, I can think of many companies similar to them I may have helped and am prepared to name drop them if appropriate. I can prepare a couple of facts about how I have been able to help those companies as well, that is, increase their conversion rates by 30%, reduce their lead costs by 25%, etc.

Step 2: Who do I actually want to speak to within the business? Who is likely to be the decision-maker?

I can look on the website, and there is normally a 'Meet the Team' page or an 'About Us' page, and within that content, there should be a name. This may not be the contact you require, but once you have a name, you can use it to get past the gatekeeper.

ME: I have been recommended to speak to John Doe, but I don't believe he is the right person. Who would you suggest I speak to regarding . . .?

The gatekeeper will be slightly more receptive than if you just said, 'Who can I speak to regarding my products and services?'

As discussed earlier, with the genius invention of LinkedIn, you can now type in a company name in the search bar and there is a tab for employees that gives you a list of many senior employees within the business.

Opening statements have a WIIFM ('What's in it for me?')

Step 3: Prepare your opening statement; this is the reason why a prospect should take your call.

When you make a call, do not tell people what you do, tell them what you have done, successfully, with companies like theirs.

Example A:

'Good morning, thanks for taking my call. My name is Tony Morris, and I am the director of the Sales Doctor. We provide bespoke training and cover an array of courses from sales to management. The reason for my call today is to see how you are developing your negotiators'.

Example B:

'Good morning Mr Estate Agent, thanks for taking my call. My name is Tony Morris and I am the director of the Sales Doctor. Are you familiar with my business?'

Yes – 'Great. As you are probably aware. . .'
OR
No – 'Allow me to introduce our company and services. . .'

'We have been successfully delivering training to many estate agents like A, B and C (name drop ones they'd have heard of) by helping negotiators qualify applicants more effectively, resulting in more qualified viewings and a significant increase in deals being tied.

'In this market, our clients have found that one of the biggest challenges they face is a lack of stock. How have you found this at the moment?

'To help our clients, we have provided the negotiators with some innovative techniques to gain more private land-lord details, and then trained them to cold call the landlords, which has resulted in an increase in valuations.

'The reason for my call today is to see if we can help your team. How are you currently developing your negotiators?'

Example B is better than the previous example, and all I did differently was briefly explain how I have helped businesses like theirs.

There may be situations where you have not helped companies in their industry. You will need to think of examples where you have helped companies that have faced similar challenges.

This happened very recently in my business, we were approached by a very big publishing company to train their 40 inbound salespeople. I knew we had not worked with companies in the publishing industry, so I found out what challenges their salespeople faced and the key areas they felt needed to be developed. Fortunately, I had trained a big tour operator who had a large inbound sales team with similar issues and challenges, and I explained very clearly what I covered with them and the benefits they received because of it.

One fundamental rule is to never lie or mislead the prospect. Do not say you have worked with a company if you haven't, because they will ring that company to ask their opinion of your goods or services. All credibility and trust are lost, and they will speak badly of your business to others.

I often get asked in my training, 'How many times should you keep trying a prospect until you give up?'

That's a great question and my answer is always the same: if you know you can help them, and that you are chasing the right contact, then you keep going until you get hold of them. Those two pieces of information need to be qualified. Confirm with as many contacts as you can, that John Doe is the person who deals with your products/services. Now many salespeople will ask for John Doe, and when told he is unavailable, they will do one of three things:

1. Is there a better time to call him? – poor question, as they'll just say, 'try again'.
2. Is he the right person who deals with a, b, and c? – poor question, because most people want you off the phone quickly, as they're busy, so you have given them an easy way out, where they'll respond, 'yes I believe he is'.

3. Is there anyone else I can speak with? – poor question, as it can lead to a no; if you don't want a no, do not ask a question that can easily lead to a no. They're most likely reply, 'not really'.

What I have observed among the top sales professionals around the globe is that they slightly tweak the question and get better responses. I call this the diamond approach.

It is always good to find out to whom John Doe reports and then you can speak to that contact, as it's much easier to get passed down than it is to be passed up. The best way to ask that is 'In John Doe's absence, who does he report too?', and then ask to speak with them. If they won't connect you, then at least you have another contact name to approach, at another time. This is the secondary goal I spoke about earlier in the book.

If the person replies that, John Doe is the key decision-maker, then ask, 'Who does he work alongside?' This might give you another one or two contacts to reach out too.

Finally, if the person says, 'He is the director and does not report to anyone or work alongside anyone', you simply say, 'Sorry to be a pain, final question, who reports directly to John?' This is your final question to try and get another contact name. If you follow this diamond approach, you are much more likely to get another contact name than if you use the three closed questions that I outlined in the earlier text.

These contacts are likely to be key influencers, and you can use them to qualify the situation, so you know whether it is worth chasing or not.

I train a courier company, whose target decision-maker is normally the MD of a small company or a warehouse manager of a larger company. They work with companies that send anywhere between 500 and 5000 domestic parcels and over two international parcels per week.

Before training, one of the sales guys had been chasing a director of a small printing company for about three months, calling him every day for the first two weeks and then every other day for the next fortnight. It then dropped off to every few days, but a lot of effort was required to keep calling him, and the time spent could have been spent on calling other businesses. Finally, the director came to the phone and said, 'Will you stop calling me? I send out about two parcels per week maximum, as 99% of my clients are local and they come and collect the parcels from my office!'

This is an easy, yet foolish, error to make. The salesperson should have qualified someone within the printing company, to get an idea of the number of parcels they send out per day, week or month. I accept that people don't always know, or are not always accurate, but I guarantee someone other than the key decision-maker will have the answers to these questions. This would have saved the salesperson from making approximately 30 unnecessary calls over a period of 12 weeks, when he could have been calling 30 other businesses that he could have helped.

On the flip side, you can get into a situation where you have the right contact, and you know you can help, but your opening gambit is so poor that you can never create an opportunity for yourself.

I personally buy many leads for my business and work with about three or four good list brokers who provide approximately 1000 leads each per month for my sales team. There is one person called Laura, who calls me towards the end of every month, just when her boss is pressuring her to hit target, no doubt, and says the same old line.

'Hi, Tony, it's your monthly call, Laura here from ABC list broker. Do you need any leads this month?'

To which I always respond, 'No, I am good. Thanks, Laura, but I will speak to you next month no doubt'.

If she stopped for a second, did her homework and made a smart call like this, her probability of a successful outcome would significantly increase:

'Good morning Tony, thanks for taking my call. It's Laura calling again from ABC list brokers. I know we have spoken many times; however, the reason for my call today is to make you aware that we have been successfully providing very high-quality leads to the top 10 sales training companies in the UK such as A, B and C, which has resulted in a significant increase in better-quality appointments for their trainers and more bookings.

'I am calling today to see if we can offer the same to you. Can I ask, where do you currently source your leads from?'

This simple opening gambit would demonstrate that Laura understood my business, has helped companies like mine and would make me stop and think for a second, as opposed to giving me an easy way out to say 'no'.

When you are calling somebody unexpected during work, you are disturbing them. They are either in a meeting, planning to go into a meeting or busy working. Therefore, when you call them, you need to make sure you engage them in the first five to ten seconds and demonstrate some value to them that will make them stop and realise that it is worth taking this call.

To help you create a powerful opening statement, look at your product/service offering and ask yourself the following questions:

1. What would a prospect **gain** from using my products/ services? That is, more efficiency, increased conversions, a more streamlined process, etc.
2. What will they reduce or avoid by using your products or services? That is, reduce their cost per lead, reduce the time to manage their system, avoid repair and maintenance costs, etc.

Once you know the key benefits that are most important to your prospect, you are able to write a powerful opening benefit statement.

Please feel free to email me your efforts at tony@ tonymorrisinternational.com and I will provide my honest feedback, with any suggestions.

Many salespeople I work with are really demotivated by the volume of calls that are needed to be made, to get hold of an influencer or a decision-maker. I view it a different way. The sales business revolves around numbers. This should be a reassuring fact, because it means, as there are some mathematics involved, there is a definite answer.

All forms of sales work on the basis of calculating how to achieve your targets through experience and ratios.

Brown and Sons specialise in selling art to large- and medium-size companies (average sale is £3000). The sales strategy is to cold call potential clients to try and organise presentations with samples and catalogues at the clients' offices.

The owner, Mr Brown, estimates that one presentation appointment will be confirmed for every 15 telephone pitches made.

On average, a sale is confirmed after three presentations. Arthur Aitken, the sales executive, has a monthly target of £30,000. Therefore, he needs an average of ten sales to achieve his target (10 × £3000).

Using Brown's estimates (three meetings = one sale), he calculates that he will need to organise 300 presentations to achieve this goal.

To make 300 meetings, using the ratios provided (15 telephone pitches = 1 meeting), he would need to make 15 × 30 telephone pitches (which totals 450).

He is working for 18 days this month, so he knows he will need to make an average of 25 pitches per day (450/18). When planning his month, Arthur must ensure he has allowed enough time to make 450 calls and present 30 pitches in addition to his other duties.

The numbers game means the structure can be put into what is a difficult task. *But it only holds true if you maintain a good attitude and enthusiasm.*

I demonstrated earlier on in this book that you can start to monitor your own conversion rates, and within a month, you'll have a very clear idea of how many calls are required to make an appointment. This will help you plan effectively. This is called reverse engineering.

Another way to view it is, how much is each call worth to you? Looking at Mr Brown's example, an average order value is £3000, and it takes him three meetings to close one sale; therefore, each meeting is worth £1000 to him. We know he needs to make 15 pitches in order to make one meeting; therefore, with every pitch he earns himself £66.67 (£1000/15). Every pitch he makes on the phone doesn't seem so demotivating, does it?

Funnelling Process

When making calls, it is important to remember the funnelling process. I was training a promotional merchandise company recently, and they would start with 500 new leads each and make cold calls.

After training, they now make smart calls and take a different approach. Once they have called all 500 leads and qualified some and left voice mails for others, they will start another 500 new leads to the mix. The issue with this is that the time they spend calling the 500 new leads, where some numbers will be dead and some will be unable to help, they could be spending that time more wisely by chasing all the warmer calls that they have funnelled from the initial 500.

When you get your initial lead bank of say 500 leads, you will call them all across your allocated times. Assuming you will not be able to help 15 of them for whatever reason, you will have 350 leads left. Out of the 350, you will leave 100 voice mails which you must follow up, you will leave your details for 100, which you have qualified and know they are now prospects as opposed to suspects, so again, these must be continuously followed up. You will then be left with 150 which you were unable to create an opportunity so far, may I add. So now you must go back to the 100 prospects to create an opportunity and the 100 people with whom you left a voice mail to qualify them as a prospect or as a suspect.

If you follow this process every time, you will not allow any to fall through the net and will increase your chances of success.

How to be 100% more effective on the telephone:

Figure 11.1

PICK IT UP!!!!

12
Direct Marketing

'If people are doubting how far you can go, go so far that you can't hear them anymore'.

—Michele Ruiz

I absolutely disagree with the 'cold calling is dead' comments; however, I do agree with warming up the prospect before making a call. This will take much more time and effort, but my late dad always said to me, 'What you put in is what you get out'.

Most people don't get mail from prospects, so you immediately stand out from your competition. And most prospects will not get lumpy mail, which will entice them to open it.

I recommend choosing a coloured envelope to match your brand colours, as it's just another way to make sure your envelope stands out.

Now, you need to decide what things will be appropriate for your prospects, but the key is to stand out, be memorable and make an impact. Here are a just few ideas to get your creative juices flowing.

One of my oldest clients is a waste-management company. One of the sales teams was speaking to a prospect and they got onto the conversation about chocolate. The prospect shared his favourite kind was Cadbury's Dairy Milk. After the call was over, Alex managed to arrange having a message to be put on a bar of Cadbury's Dairy Milk, as seen in Figure 12.1.

Figure 12.1

To take this to another level, she placed in her blue envelope, which is her brand colour, a small dustbin, as they manage waste. And the message read, 'Please put the wrapper in the bin provided, we take waste very seriously' (Figure 12.2).

Figure 12.2

Funny enough, when Alex called back, the prospect agreed to a meeting within the first 20 seconds of the call. He said to Alex that he has never been more impressed with an outreach approach in his 37 years in business and it has inspired him to get his sales team to think differently.

One brand I have always wanted to get in with is Specsavers. They are one of the largest opticians in the UK, with hundreds of stores. I have had success in this industry working with the Luxottica Group and training the sales team at Oakley sunglasses.

My VA found eight people that she felt could be the stakeholders. She got all their contact details, including their work postal address. So, rather than me picking up the phone and doing a cold call, I decided to warm the prospects up. In order to think about what the right thing was to send them, I thought about what their biggest pain is most likely to be. I know most opticians need to get more prospects in for eye tests, because if the optometrists deal with them the right way, that prospect will become a customer.

This is what I created: I chose to send a typed letter in size 6 font. I placed the letter inside a blue envelope, my brand colour, and inserted a small magnifying glass, as seen in Figure 12.3. The letter said the following:

Dear NAME,

If you need to use a magnifying glass to read this, you need your eyes tested.

We have successfully helped over 23 opticians and retailers, the likes of the Luxottica Group. We have helped them generate more eye tests, by out-of-the-box thinking, and helped them convert more eye tests into clients.

Please call me on the number mentioned on my business card, if you would like to learn how we can help Specsavers generate more eye tests, win more clients and increase the average order value.

Alternatively, I will be in touch over the next few days to discuss this in depth.

Look forward to hearing from you.

Kindest regards,

Tony

Figure 12.3

On the back of this going out, my sales teams are now following up to book appointments for my team and me.

One industry that we have had a lot of success in is 'SaaS' (software as a service). When I was thinking about what to send them, I really struggled, as they have a variety of pains and I didn't want to pinpoint just one, as it may not have been relevant. So I thought about a general item that will stand out, make them laugh and warm them up for a call. This is what I produced (Figure 12.4).

Figure 12.4

The letter read:

Dear NAME,

Now I have my foot in the door.

We have successfully helped over 37 businesses, the likes of Syft, Inspect Real Estate, Spectre, to name a few. We helped their sales teams triple the number of appointments they generated for their BDMs, resulting in a significant increase of revenue for the business.

If you would like your BDMs on more appointments, then please contact me on the phone number mentioned on my business card and it would be great to hear from you.

Alternatively, my team will be in touch in the next few days to see if we can help you, like we helped our other SaaS clients.

Kindest regards,

Tony Morris

Tonymorrisinternational.com

Another industry we serve is estate agents. Having helped over 250 of them, their continuous pain is not having enough properties to sell or let. Without property, they have no businesses.

Therefore, I knew I had to come up with an idea to demonstrate we help estate agents get more properties to sell or let. And this was my idea (Figure 12.5).

Figure 12.5

I typed a letter, folded it, put a few monopoly houses inside the letter and placed it in a blue envelope. When the prospect had opened the letter, the houses would have fallen onto the floor. The letter read:

Dear NAME,

We can help you generate a number of instructions, in the next three weeks, without spending an extra penny on marketing.

We have successfully helped over 237 estate and letting agents, the likes of Manning Stainton, Webbers, Marsh & Parsons, to name a few, by tripling their valuations, within 12 weeks, without spending an extra penny on marketing.

If you would like to learn my #1 strategy of how we do this, enter this URL Calendly.com/tony-morris/call, and book a Zoom meeting, where I will share this strategy with you.

Alternatively, please give a ring on the phone number mentioned on my business card and it would be great to hear from you.

Alternatively, my team will be in touch in the next few days to see if we can help you, like we helped so many other estate agents.

Kindest regards,

Tony

Finally, we do a lot of work in the financial services industry, specifically IFAs, mortgage and protection advisers, etc. Again, they have a variety of pains, so it's difficult to pinpoint which one is the most painful for them. When you're in that predicament, you are better to choose something that stands out and still makes the point of being that little bit different. This idea is ideal if budgets are small, but you still want to warm the prospect up.

You get an A4 envelope, again the colour of your brand, type a letter and put it into a ball (Figure 12.6).

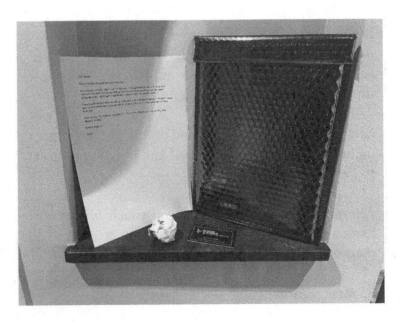

Figure 12.6

When the prospect opens the letter, it reads:

Dear NAME,

This is the only thing we will ever screw up.

We have successfully helped over 23 IFAs and mortgage advisers, working the largest networks, the likes of MAB, by helping them sell more protection with more mortgage cases, resulting in a significant increase in revenue on their cases.

If you would also like your advisers selling more protection, with the mortgages they write, please contact me on the phone number mentioned on my business card and it would be great to hear from you.

Alternatively, my team will be in touch in the next few days to see if we can help your advisers as well.

Kindest regards,

Tony

There is no guarantee you are going to book appointment or get a positive response from the prospect even after all this; however, you have a better chance than someone who just picks up the phone and makes a cold call.

The key is to pick up the phone and call the prospect, until you reach them. Remember, 'the fortune is in the follow-up'.

13
I Only Have Capacity for Seven Clients

'We need to accept that we won't always make the right decisions, that we'll screw up royally sometimes; understand that failure is not the opposite of success, it's part of success'.

—Arianna Huffington

I was scrolling Facebook one evening, and came across this post by a guy called Jonathan Jay. He said, 'This year, I only have the capacity to take on seven clients. To see if you could be one of those seven, please read this. . .'.

This caught my attention, and I read on.

He started talking a little about his journey; he set up a coaching company called 'The Coaching Academy' and sold it for £28 million.

Now I was really engaged.

He said, 'To make an application to see if you're the right fit, please fill in this form'.

I printed out this six-page form, made myself a cup of tea and started to fill it out. It asked questions like, 'Do you have the ambition to make a turnover of £1 million a year'. 'Yeah, I do', I thought to myself.

'Do you want to expand overseas and enter new markets?' 'Absolutely', I wrote.

'Do you want to learn how to stand on stage and deliver an offer so compelling that 70% of the audience will run to the back of the room to sign up?' 'That would be unreal', I wrote.

'Do you want to learn how to write a book and be an Amazon bestseller within 12 months?' I was scribbling through this form with so much excitement.

And then it suddenly dawned on me. I am applying to see if I am one of the lucky seven to be chosen to be coached by Jonathan Jay. This guy is a genius. He's sold to me, and I didn't even see it. I felt like I was under hypnosis without a teacher.

I decided to complete the form, as I was two-thirds of the way through it and I wanted to see how this played out. I emailed my form off and got an automatic response thanking me for my application. Ha! he thinks he's got me, and I am not falling for it.

About three days later I got an email that read:

Subject line: Tony, we have read your application

Dear Tony,

Firstly, thank you for taking the time to fill out this application. This first part of the selection process is called 'The Filter'. We know only about 15% of people take the time to complete the application, and Jonathan only works with people who are 100% committed.

As you can imagine, although only 15% complete it, we have been inundated with the application. Which is why it's taken us a few days to get back to you.

We have read all your answers and we are afraid you have not met our criteria.

We thank you again for taking the time and we wish you every success.

Kind regards,
Michael

A consultant for Jonathan Jay International

0845. . . .

I wasn't selected! I was livid. Why not? What was wrong with me?

I immediately called this Michael guy to give him a peace of my mind. I spent over an hour answering those questions, and I got rejected.

MICHAEL:	Thanks for calling Jonathan Jay International, Michael speaking, how can I help?
ME:	Yes, hi Michael, it's Tony Morris here.
MICHAEL:	Hi Tony, what can I do for you?
ME:	I just got an email from you about my application to look at working with Jonathan Jay, and it said that I was rejected. I just wanted to understand why.
MICHAEL:	Firstly, thank you for taking the time to get in touch.

This was the second part of our filtering process. Jonathan knows that only 7% of people take the time to call on receipt of the rejection email and you're one of those 7%.

ME (THINKING):	Damn, he got me again. I was starting to really dislike this guy. But he was a sales Jedi.

MICHAEL: In order to qualify, Jonathan would like to give you 20 minutes of his time, to ask you a few further questions to ensure you really are the right fit for him. Looking at his diary, he's available on the 24th March at 16:45 or 2nd April at 11:15, which one works for you?

ME: That's like three weeks away. Has he not got anything earlier?

MICHAEL: I'm afraid that's his first availability.

ME: Let's go for 24th March in that case.

MICHAEL: I'll send you a meeting invite after this call, and please accept this invite into your diary, otherwise Jonathan will not attend the appointment.

ME: Yes, no problem at all.

MICHAEL: Thanks again for calling, and have a great day.

As the line went dead, I thought about our call and realised, I'd just been done again! Not available for three weeks? Or was he this busy and this was all genuine?

I was so intrigued to find out that I accepted the meeting into my diary.

24th March came around very quickly and at 11:30 am that day I got a call from Michael.

ME: Tony speaking.
MICHAEL: Tony, it's Michael here from Jonathan
            Jays' team.
ME: Hi Michael, is this just to confirm my
            appointment with Jonathan later today?
MICHAEL: I'm so sorry, but Jonathan has had to take
            a flight to the States for an urgent meeting
            and cannot make the meeting. He sends
            his sincerest apologies.
ME: That's ridiculous, I've been waiting
            three weeks for the meeting. When is
            he free?
MICHAEL: As he has inconvenienced you, he can do
            this Thursday at 18:30 your time, which
            will be 13:30 his time in the States.
ME: Bear with me; yes, I can make that work.
MICHAEL: Thank you so much for your understand-
            ing and accommodating us, have a great
            rest of your day.

    Thursday 26th March at 18:29, I got a call on
my mobile.

ME: Tony speaking.
JONATHAN: Tony, it's Jonathan Jay here. How are you?
ME: I'm good, thanks.
JONATHAN: Firstly, can I just congratulate you?
ME: What for?
JONATHAN: You passed.
ME: Passed what?

JONATHAN: Only 2% of people agree to reschedule the meeting at such a short notice, and you're part of that 2%. This was the final part of our filtering process, as you've shown us how committed you are to achieving your goals. What I'd like to do on this call is peel off the onion a little bit and get to know you and make sure we can work together. Is that okay with you?

ME: You had me at 'only'. Where do I need to sign? I'm in!

This concept was used again, but this time in a face-to-face interaction.

I was introduced to a guy called Graeme Godfrey. I was told he was a life coach, and I emailed him and we set up a call. On that call, he asked me a couple of questions, about what I thought my biggest issue was and he just listened. He then said, 'I don't think that's your issue'. I was so intrigued, I said, 'Then what's my issue?'

He said, 'Let's meet, as I want to discuss it in person, and have a chat and ask you a few more questions'.

I said, 'I'm happy to meet, but can you tell me exactly what you do and what you charge?'

He said, 'I coach people to have the life they dream of, but have got themselves a little lost, and I help them find their way again. I have a few different ways, I help clients, and it's best that we meet and once I understand more, I can then see if I am able to help, and then discuss the right program and the costs involved'.

I shared my current coach's cost, and he said, 'I'm nothing like that and my fees are going to hurt you.' He said, 'No need to discuss fees now, as after our discovery meeting I may not be able to work with you anyway'. Then he closed a meeting.

We met at my house and very quickly he got me talking about me for one hour (everyone loves to talk about themselves, so he made me feel good and showed he cares).

He then said, 'I am very selective with whom I mentor, and I'm going to ask you some uncomfortable questions and want to make sure you're okay with that?'

I said, 'Yes, that's fine'.

He asked, 'Tell me about the first trauma you remember'.

I told him a story about when I was 14 years old and my Yorkshire terrier called Rocky got attacked by an Alsatian. He noted this all down, and I saw he put a circle around 14.

Then he asked about my second traumatic event, and I told him about losing my dad. 'Tell me about it', he said, and I went into detail, as although it was 16 years ago, I remember it like it was yesterday.

And then he asked about the biggest trauma since setting up my business. I thought trauma was an interesting word and a very emotive word.

I was aware that these questions were done in chronological order according to my age, which is easy for people to process and then he stacked my traumas up to the point I was close to tears.

He then said, 'If you were coaching yourself, what would you say to yourself?'

I said, 'You're carrying around a lot of stress, you have not dealt with a lot of stuff in your past and they're holding you back'.

He said, 'There you are then.' I realised that he got me to diagnose the pain, which was very clever.

He said, 'You are not fulfilling your huge potential, because you're holding so much back'.

He went on to ask me what my goals were and why those goals in particular.

Once I shared financial goals, he asked, 'What have I done so far regarding the provisions for those savings?'

I said, 'Nothing', and he said, 'Your goals are dreams with no strategy'.

This was a very clever way of making me see that I had not found the way to achieve my goals and, therefore, I really needed his help.

When I said, 'My end goal is to have £5 million in my bank to retire'. He questioned why that amount? And once I explained, he then proved that I needed so much more, with the life I want to live. He asked why am I aiming so low?

This gave me the impression he believed I can achieve so much more.

He then said, 'When you get there, what do you think would happen?'

I said, 'I'd celebrate and play tennis every day and go on three weekend breaks a month with Shana and spend more time with the kids'.

Again, this was a great technique to get me to imagine what my dream life could look like and how I would feel if I got there.

He gave a personal story, explaining he thought he would do the same when he retired at 49, and after four months he got bored of golf and racket ball and got back into business.

People love a personal story, and what it did was build his credibility, as he retired at 49, showing he was successful and that if he can do it, then I too can do it.

He shared that he is very private about his clients, but because he has had such an impact on their lives, they insisted on doing a testimonial for him and he suggested I look at them.

Again, a clever way of positioning it for me to be intrigued to hear what his clients have to say about him.

He then said at the end of the meeting, 'You remind me of a younger version of myself'.

This gave me a good feeling, as I too could retire at 49. And it's great to leave your prospective customer feeling good.

He gave me homework.

1. Three words to describe your best life.
2. Three words to describe your worst life.
3. Explain how you arrived at those words.

He gave me a deadline of Friday (five days later).

I texted him my answers on Tuesday night and he said, 'You've passed my first test that I didn't tell you about. This shows how committed you are to this process'.

We then had another meeting, this time on Zoom. We talked through my answers to the test and his interpretations of them, which I thought were really interesting. And then he said, 'Tony, I have no question in my mind whether I can help you'.

'It's just a case of whether you want to be helped.'

I said, 'of course I want to be helped, that's why I came to you'.

He said, 'Okay then. But you have to be "all in", or this doesn't work'.

I said, 'I'm all in'.

He said, 'I think I can help you faster than you realise'.

He said, 'Many of my clients need me for six months, but I actually think I can help you in three to four months'.

I realised this was a great technique. He demonstrated he didn't care about the money; it was all about helping the client.

I then said, 'How much are we talking?'

Before he even answered, I remember thinking to myself, 'I hope I can afford him'. Wouldn't it be amazing if we could get every prospect to think that to themselves?

He shared his price and explained he only works face to face and does 2 × 2 hours a month.

I remember calculating his hourly rate and thinking he was unaffordable. And I was genuinely gutted, because I knew he could help, but I didn't want to start building debt in order to work with him.

I said, 'I really would love to work with you, but I just cannot afford it'.

I was expecting him to put up a fight or move a little on his fees, and he said, 'I understand. When you're ready, let's speak again, as it really would be great to work with you'.

And that was it.

I spoke to Shana about him and said, 'I really want to do it, what do you think'. She agreed it's a lot of money, but we have more than enough in our savings, and she said we are investing in our future, so let's do it.

I called Graeme back a few days later and said, 'I really want to work with you, but it's a lot of money. Is there any way we can do a deal, where you earn a commission on the results you help me get?'

He said, 'It's not how I work. It needs to be painful for you to make sure you are all in'.

This made total sense to me.

But it made me want it even more. Again, a genius at work.

My final ask was, 'What if I gave you a percentage of my business?' And he replied, 'That would be an error on your side, and when you learn what I'll teach you, you would regret giving me any of your business'.

With that, he had me. And like Jonathan Jay, I'd been sold twice, by two of the best sales professionals I've ever encountered.

However, Jonathan helped me grow and changed my perspective on marketing.

And as I write this, I am four months into my time with Graeme and it's been worth every penny.

14
Questioning

'The harder I work, the luckier I get'.

—Gary Player

One of the most important parts of sales is questioning. The better your questioning, the better understanding you get of your prospects' needs, and therefore, giving you the best chance of recommending the right products/services to them.

So, why do we ask open-ended questions?

- To gain information.
- To show an interest in your prospect/customer.
- To make them comfortable.
- To be thorough.
- To build rapport.
- To get your prospect/customer to talk (80/20).

Compare the following:

DOCTOR 1:

ME: Doctor, I hope you can help, I have a splitting headache.

DOCTOR 1: Take some paracetamol, and if the pain persists, please come back to see me.

DOCTOR 2:

ME: I hope you can help, I have a splitting headache.

DOCTOR 2: Where exactly is the pain?

ME: In my temples.

DOCTOR 2: What time do you usually get these headaches?

ME: Normally the morning.

DOCTOR 2: How long have you been suffering?

ME: About a month.

DOCTOR 2: How much water do you drink per day?

ME: About a litre, I guess.

DOCTOR 2: On a scale of 1 to 10, 10 being excruciating pain, where would you describe your pain?

ME: I suppose a 7 at its worst.

DOCTOR 2: From what you've described, I would recommend paracetamol, but if the pain persists, come back, and see me.

Which doctor would you rather see?
I assume the latter would be your answer.
Which doctor is better medically trained?

We don't really know; they could be as qualified as each other.

So why did you choose Doctor 2?

What did the second doctor demonstrate that the first doctor didn't?

The doctor showed their credibility, clearly took an interest in me and gave me absolute confidence that they knew what they were doing. So by asking a few open-ended questions to the patient, I made a perception that Doctor 2 was far more professional and a much better doctor (Figure 14.1).

What's the best way to remember the open-ended questions?

Figure 14.1

'I keep six honest serving men, they taught me all I knew; their names are What and Why and When and How and Where and Who' (Rudyard Kipling, *Just So Stories*).

For the visual readers, I would recommend Figure 14.2, which is described as the 'six bottoms on a rugby post'. The bottoms represent the six Ws and the bench representing the H for How.

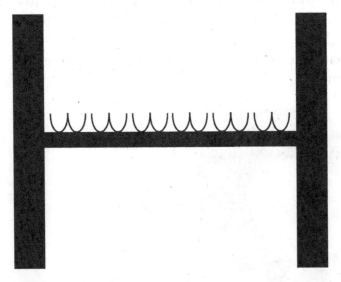

Figure 14.2

These types of questions should necessitate the client's participation in the conversation. This results in the client's attention being directed to you and away from any previous activity.

Here are some examples of the open-ended questions:

'What in, your opinion, is the most effective way of marketing your company?'
'Why do you believe this is the case?'
'How would you like to see your marketing develop?'

Open-ended questions ensure that the dialogue becomes less of a sales pitch and more of a conversation, as you have shown genuine interest in their opinion and views.

Here are some open question techniques I have developed and learned over the years I have been in sales. They have to be used for different purposes and at different parts of the sales conversation, which I will elaborate on.

Tag-On Questions

As with everyday conversations, these questions are a response to the person's reply to your initial open question.
For example:

Question – Where do you come from?
Answer – From Bournemouth, in Dorset.
Question – How did you like living in Bournemouth?

This follow-up question has shown that you listened to the previous answer and now wish to get the person to expand further.

Statement Question

To get actively involved in dialogue and make it a conversation, NOT an interrogation, I suggest the statement question. Quite simply, make a statement and follow it up with an open question: 'I have never actually visited Bournemouth; however, I have heard lots of lovely things about it. What drew you there in the first place?'

Opinion Question

Some people like to give their opinion, especially if they have some knowledge on the subject, so let them. By allowing that person to talk, they will feel comfortable, and therefore more likely to warm to you, and want to work with you. One easy way to create this scenario is by asking, 'What's your opinion on. . .?'

I have observed many estate agents as when they are valuing a person's property, and they know the person has lived there for a few years, they would ask, 'You have been living here from past X years, what's your opinion on the current situation of the market, compared to when you moved here?' Then the estate agent zips up and lets the seller talk.

Replay Question

There is no value in asking questions and not listening to the answers. This was something I was certainly guilty of when I was a teenager. Earlier, I found myself getting distracted easily while listening to someone, and knowing that listening is arguably the most fundamental aspect of sales, I have worked so hard at developing this specific skill set.

One of the most effective ways to demonstrate to a person that you have been listening to them is ask them an open question about something they said earlier in the conversation; for example, 'How old were you when you actually moved to Bournemouth?'

Clarification Question

When a person uses vague language, its vital that you ask a clarification question to ensure you get a better understanding of what they mean. Remember, we all have a slightly different lens.

PROSPECT: I really need this solved quickly.
YOU: That's fine, but just to understand, what do you deem as quickly?

Future Pace Question

When I am in a sales meeting, and I am probing to understand a prospect's challenges and goals, I would ask them a statement question like, 'If we decide to work with one another, what is your number one objective?' I found that 98% of prospects would have exactly the same response, which was, 'To increase sales'. I thought to myself, although I am there to discuss developing their sales team, it is not possible that everyone has exactly the same goal.

If you ask a question, and don't get the right response, then change the question.

I changed the question to a future pace question. For example, 'Imagine we fast forward six months from today, how do you know my training has been successful?'

This generated so many different responses, such as:

'We have seen a significant boost in morale across the team'.

'My teams' call activity has gone through the roof'.

'I have seen our conversion rates, from an enquiry to a sale, go up by 17%'.

Changing the question was so thought-provoking that it caused the prospect to really dig deep and highlight their 'real' motivation. Once I understood that and my competitors didn't, the probability of me securing the business increased.

Pain Questions

These are one of the most effective types of questions. We know that prospects are 2.5 times more motivated to act to solve a problem. Therefore, your questions need to be heavily focused on eliciting problems, challenges and issues. The bigger the pain, the more likely the prospect is to take action.

Here are some examples of pain questions, in response to a prospect saying, 'I am happy with my current supplier'.

Question: 'I appreciate that; if there was just one area that they could do better, what would that one area be?'

Question: 'If you had to rate their service levels, ten being they are exceptional and one being they are dreadful, where do you rate them? And what would make them a ten?'

Question: 'What improvements would you like to see in the solution?'

Benchmarking Question

In the last example, if the prospects say, 'I am really happy with my current supplier', and they answer very positively to the pain questions, then you move into the benchmarking question. You say the following, 'I understand you've been working with X company for five years now; when did you last benchmark them, to ensure you're getting the highest-quality service and paying the right price?' If they have not been through a benchmark process, this might open up a door of opportunity for you.

Decision-Maker Questions

This is a vital part of the sales process and an area most salespeople get wrong. I recall a conversation I had many years ago, with an MD of a health and safety company. During the conversation I said to David, 'As the MD,

I assume it will be your decision?', and he replied, 'It certainly would be'. I booked a meeting, for the next few days. I spent a couple of hours preparing for the meeting and then two and a half hours to drive to the meeting. We had a great meeting for over an hour and my discovery questions were on point, I qualified the opportunity and then made my recommendation. When I went to close the deal by saying, 'So, it all makes sense to me, does it make sense to you?' He replied, 'Absolutely'. I said, 'Great, when would you like to kick the training off?' He responded, 'Well, I need to run things through my business partner Brad'.

I was thinking, who's Brad? Why didn't he tell me about this Brad? Because I asked the wrong question. Had I asked, 'Aside from yourself, who else gets involved in making the decision?', he would have told me, 'Myself, and my business partner Brad'. To this, I would have responded with what I call a 'justification statement' – 'It is important I meet both Brad and you, as I feel business partners tend to ask different questions and I want to be able to answer those, so that together you can make a joint decision. Looking at my diary, I can meet you both on next Wednesday at 15:45 p.m. or Friday at 09:15 a.m.; which time suits you both best?'

During the meeting, I would then have asked, 'What are your key priorities in order to make this decision?'

Thought-Provoking Questions

As the name suggests, these types of questions are used to get your prospect really thinking. By doing so, they are much more likely to really open and share things that they might otherwise not have shared.

Some example questions:

'I understand that most of your business comes from your four main clients, correct?'

'What would you do if you lost them?'

'What processes do you have in place to keep them?'

Discovery Questions

Finally, we get to discovery questions. These are the most important set of questions to truly qualify a sales opportunity. In essence, they are a combination of the different questioning types I have just run through with you.

Here are a few examples of discovery questions if you were selling waste management in a B2B environment:

1. When did you last review your waste management?
2. What's the reason you are reviewing it at present?
3. How do you benchmark you current service levels?
4. What specific aspects are you reviewing?
5. When choosing a waste management partner, what are your five key priorities?
6. How often does your current supplier communicate with you? How often would you like them to?
7. What are you not getting that you would like?
8. On a scale of 1–10, 10 being exceptional service, how would you rate your current supplier? What's required to make it a 10?
9. What products/services do you have with your current supplier?

10. How important is to you to have aesthetically pleasing containers? (only ask this if you have noticed their containers are in poor condition)
11. When did your current supplier last let you down? What impact did this have on your business? What recycling activities do you currently operate?

Why Do We Ask Closed-Ended Questions?

Now we move into closed questions. These are questions that can only get a 'yes' and 'no' response. Like open-ended questions, these are used at different steps of the sales process.

So, why do we ask closed-ended questions?

To clarify certain points – 'Am I right in saying that you need delivery after 5 p.m.?'

To get confirmation – 'You'll need 200 printed in colour and in size A5, is that correct?'

To close a prospect – 'Would you like to go ahead? Would you like to move this forward?'

If the prospect hesitates at the closing questions, you then use an open question to uncover their reservations. Tell me, 'What's causing you to hesitate?'

To gain commitment – 'If I can agree a payment schedule, over a three-month period and delivery within 72 hours, can I have your business today?'

My recommendation is you and your sales team brainstorm all the key things you need to ascertain from a prospect, in order to qualify or disqualify them, and then you design the questions around those concerns.

15
Listening

'Energy flows where energy grows – focus on what you want, not what you don't want'.

—Tony Robbins

I mentioned at the beginning of this book about Pareto's law that as a sales professional, we should be listening 80% of the time and only speaking 20% of the time. Although this is the ideal model, in reality, it can be challenging, especially when the prospect has many questions for you. So there are ways to practice and develop your listening, as it's a skill in itself.

A Smart Salesperson Listens to Emotions, Not Facts

Imagine an iceberg when describing communication: only about 20% of the iceberg is visible, and 80% is below the surface. When you listen to facts, you are hearing 20% of what someone is communicating to you. When you listen to emotions, you are paying attention to the other 80%.

Listen to what is *not* said, that is, if a client says, 'I can't use this product', is the prospect saying they do not know how to use it, they do not want to use it or they have another product in mind?

If a client says, 'We have found such systems don't work very well' Who are 'we'? What does work well? What has worked better in the past?

Limit the Time You Speak

Research has shown that prospects have an attention span that lasts about 30 seconds. TV advertisers have known for a long time that if their ads last more than 30 seconds, people will go for a cup of coffee or change the channel. As a rule, never talk for more than 30–45 seconds without asking, 'Any comments about this? What are your thoughts so far? Any questions?'

Reflective Listening

This is repeating some words your client or prospect uses to demonstrate you have been listening, that is, if a prospect is describing a challenge that the sales team is facing around time management and they say, 'avoiding time thieves', you then ask a question later on, 'What strategies have you got in place to help your sales team avoid the time thieves?'

Tag-On Questions

As I mentioned earlier, this is one of the most effective ways to demonstrate that you are listening, and develop your listening skills. If the person says, 'I really enjoyed my holiday in Italy', your response should be, 'Which part of Italy did you visit?'

I receive approximately five cold calls per week. The majority are poor, with an unclear or non-existent opening gambit. As I run a training company, this is an ideal lead opportunity for me. I found out from the telesales person who their boss was and then did a quick smart call to create an opportunity to sell sales training. One cold call I received a few years back shows a much bigger opportunity was missed by the salesperson when a guy called me from a mobile phone company.

The call went something like this:

SALESMAN:	Good morning, Tony. My name is Steve Berry from XPhones and I'm calling to find out about your mobile phone. I'd like to know if you have a contract in place. Can I ask, do you have a mobile?
ME:	Yes, I have a Blackberry.
SALESPERSON:	Great, and are you in a contract?

ME:	Yes, I am. Why are you asking me these questions?
SALESPERSON:	To see if I can reduce your bill and get you a better mobile, how long do you have left on your contract?
ME:	We have about eight months left and are happy with the Blackberry phones. Do me a favour; I am really busy, so call me in about seven to eight months. When our contract is up for renewal we can discuss this further.

Although there was no rapport, no great opening gambit and awfully prepared closed-ended questions, did you pick up on the one or two words that Steve clearly missed to create a much bigger opportunity?

Steve was clearly focused on selling me a mobile and a new contract, so he blocked out or distorted the words I used. I mentioned 'we have' about eight months left, and I pluralised 'phone'. Steve should have questioned me about the plurals, and I would have told him that I have a sales force of eight with a corporate contract in place. He could have easily hit me with a great benefit statement such as, 'We specialise in corporate contracts and have been able to significantly reduce a company's monthly bills by over 40% when a company has five or more handsets. What I suggest is meeting you to find more about your deal and seeing if we are able to buy you out of your contract. I am available Tuesday and Thursday next week, please let me know which one suits you best?'

A good listener needs to do more than hear what the other person is saying, they need to evaluate and interpret it. This is known as active listening, because it enables you to react to, and lead, the conversation.

Too often, valuable information is lost through not listening when important facts are introduced.

Improving Active Listening Skills

Listening skills in sales are developed in exactly the same way as listening skills in everyday life. There are a number of ways in which listening ability can be improved.

Clarification

It is vital that you clarify something when you are not certain that you understand a point. This shows that you are listening and that you have understood everything that has been said. Ask for an explanation, if necessary, for example, 'You said that your budget was "time-sensitive". What does that mean, exactly?'

Confirmation

When a client expresses a need that you know your product can help with, allow the client to confirm the point. This will not only enable you to understand the subject better, but also to reaffirm the problem in the client's mind, so they will be more receptive to your product, for example, 'Did your responses really drop by 20% last year?'

Nonverbal

It is harder to maintain good listening skills when you can't see the speaker. Both parties are vulnerable to outside influences and distractions. It can be helpful to imagine that you are face to face to implement some of the following techniques:

Appropriate body language – leaning forward when discussing important or confidential subjects.

Nodding or shaking the head to indicate a reaction to what is said.

Warm and open smile – people can hear this on the phone.

This will raise your concentration and make you a more effective listener. No one likes talking to silence, so making acknowledgment sounds, such as mmm, sure, yup, I see, etc., gives the talker comfort that you are listening to them.

As a sales professional, one key thing we need to be listening out for is what's called 'buying signals'. These are signs of interest from a prospective customer. Good examples of these could be if the prospect asks:

'What's the minimum term of a contract with your company?'

'How much are your services for?'

'How did you help my competition?'
'What experience have you got in our industry?'
'How can we monitor the results?'

The prospect would not ask any of these questions unless there was an appetite there. Our job is to answer these questions and find out the reason behind the question. This will identify what's important to the prospective customer and then we can control the conversation. Many salespeople miss these signals, go off on a tangent and start telling the prospect things that do not interest or are of no relevance to them.

Opportunity Antenna

Having now helped over 36,000 salespeople, I started to realise what the top 1% had in common. It wasn't that they were just better at selling, they had this ability to hear things that were not even shared. I call this, your 'opportunity antenna'.

I was training an estate agent in East Croydon who was struggling for ideas to get valuations. Because without valuations, they can't win instructions (properties), and if they have no properties, they have no business. As a team, we were brainstorming marketing ideas.

We were talking about how well-known they are in their local community. And one of the team members said that his dad is friends with the owner of one of the coffee shops in Crystal Palace. I said, 'You should give them 50 branded mugs, so the locals will see your brand every time they have a coffee there'. I asked how his dad knew him, and he explained his dad is a keen cyclist and part of a massive cyclist club. He went on to say that every week approximately 200 cyclists meet on Sunday at that coffee shop. As I heard, '200 local cyclists', my opportunity antenna started bleeping. As they're part of a local cyclist club and stop for coffee at the local coffee shops, one could assume that many of them must be locals.

I looked at the team waiting for someone to shout it out. But silence. I could not hold it in any longer and I shouted out, 'Hand out branded water bottles that fit on their bike racks'. That way, it's on them every time they cycle. And every time they stop, there is no guarantee they'll do business, but if they don't do it, then there is a guarantee that they won't.

Listening to What Is 'Not' Shared

I was working with a car-leasing company, which does personal contract hire and corporate fleets. I was listening to one of the sales team members called Max and this is a summary of how I remember the call:

MAX: Welcome to X car leasing, Max speaking.
PROSPECT: Hi there, my name is Lisa and I'm looking to lease a new car and was hoping you could help.
MAX: Absolutely, I can. Out of curiosity, who recommended you to X car leasing?

PROSPECT: I found you online.

MAX: Good stuff. The only reason I ask is that most of our business is recommended. Tell me, what's brought you to leasing?

PROSPECT: I've just been offered a new job, and I start in six weeks and need a new car before then.

MAX: Congrats on the job and am sure we can accommodate that time frame. Do you know how the leasing process works?

PROSPECT: Yes, I do. I've not leased before but my husband leases his car at work.

MAX: Good stuff. Tell me, what car do you have in mind?

PROSPECT: I'd love a BMW. I have two kids, so can't get a two-seater, but my husband has a jeep, so would rather something else, and want it to look sporty; nothing too fast though.

MAX: Okay, there are a few options. What budget do you have?

PROSPECT: I've been given £450 a month car allowance.

MAX: That's a good amount, and we can get you something nice. Let me just ask you some details about the car itself. What features are important to you?

PROSPECT: I'm not looking for all the bells and whistles. Just need satnav, reverse camera and alloys. And ideally black or white.

MAX: Okay, we can do all of that. Based on what you've told me, I think the M4 sport could work. It's not got the engine size of an

	M4, but it's sporty, ideal for kids, and we can get it in white in the next five weeks.
PROSPECT:	Sounds great.
MAX:	Now just the boring stuff. Petrol, mileage, payment terms, etc., and finally, would you like maintenance?
PROSPECT:	No thanks. My brother is a mechanic, so if there are any issues, he can sort it.
MAX:	Good stuff. What I'll do now is go to the market and look at the best deals we have available. Let me take down your email and I'll send you some options, and let's discuss tomorrow.

The call went down. Max did his research, sent Lisa a quote with three options and called her back the following day.

PROSPECT:	Lisa speaking.
MAX:	Lisa, it's Max, calling as promised.
PROSPECT:	Yes, hi Max. Thanks for calling back. I had a look, and I'd like to order the first option, please. It suits me over two years, and putting one month down, and if you promise it will be here in five weeks, I'm good to go.
MAX:	That's great Lisa and you have my word. We have them in stock, and I'll reserve it after this call.

Max took her card details for the deposit and address details. He thanked her for calling X leasing and hung up the phone.

He looked at me and said, 'I'm great, aren't I?'

I said, 'You're excellent, but you missed two things'. Any ideas, Max?

He didn't have a clue on what he missed.

Before I divulge, did you notice what he missed?

There were two misses and one of them was a game changer.

Opportunity 1:

I know how leasing works. I've not leased, but my **husband leases** with **his company.**

Max should have got details about the jeep Lisa's husband leases. What jeep is it? When is the lease up for renewal? And then he should have found out about his company. Does he work for someone or does he employ people, and if so, do they have leased vehicles?

Opportunity 2 (the bigger one):

What's your budget? My **company** has given me a £450 a month car allowance.

This did not even dawn on Max. If Lisa is given a £450 monthly allowance, is it fair to assume other staff would have also been given one?

The day after the call, Max called Lisa back and told her the car has been ordered. He then asked her, 'Lisa you mentioned your company has given you a car allowance of £450 per month, how many other employees are there at your company?

LISA: I am not sure exactly, as I have not started yet; however, I would guess around 3000. Once Max had picked himself off the floor and got back on his seat, he asked, 'When you start, would you be so kind to introduce me to your HR director, as I would love to learn how many other employees are given a car allowance'.

LISA: Yes, I am more than happy to do that for you, once I have started.

It took Max about two months to arrange a meeting with the HR director. He met her, along with the MD of the car-leasing company. Last year, they ordered 360 vehicles for their staff. Max earned in excess of £20,000 for that deal. He did not even get me a bottle of wine, the BASketball player.

Listen to Learn

I mentioned earlier in this book that 99% of salespeople 'listen to respond'. As the prospect or client is speaking, they are thinking when is it their time to speak?

The top 1% of salespeople listen to learn. Here is an example to illustrate this.

I was working with an independent estate agency in York, North of England. I was out with a valuer called George, who was meeting the seller called Sarah at her property quite close to the city centre. As we arrived, the lady explained she could only give us 30 minutes maximum, as she was running a little late for work. George said, 'That's absolutely fine, we can make that work'. Once Sarah had shown us round the property, we sat down in the lounge and George was opening his iPad to show Sarah a quick presentation. As he was doing so, I asked Sarah, 'Out of curiosity, what do you do for work?' She replied, 'I run an antenatal business here in the city centre'. 'Fantastic', I said. I loved my antenatal classes, as I had no idea how to even put a nappy on a baby.

George opened his iPad to show Sarah the brief presentation of the estate agency. He went through it, answered Sarah's questions, gave her a valuation of the property and organised to call the following day to arrange next steps, as he could see she was in a rush.

We got in his car, and he asked for my feedback. I said, 'You did a great job however, you missed something'.

Any idea of what he missed?

I run antenatal classes here in the city centre. One of the biggest reasons people move properties is they are having a family and therefore need to upsize. George did not even pick up the point that Sarah ran an antenatal class in the city centre. The following day, George called Sarah and she instructed him to sell her property. He went on to ask about her antenatal classes, and organised to come to one of her classes and meet her members. It only took a couple of weeks, and George booked three valuations on the back of that meeting.

Remember, you have two ears and one mouth. You need to use them in that order.

16
As Nike Says, 'Just Do It'

'Things may come to those who wait, but only the things that are left by those who hustle'.

—Abraham Lincoln

When I self-published the first edition of this book, it was my dream to get it into WHSmith, which is one of the largest book retailers in the UK. I knew this was going to be a huge challenge, as I had no publisher helping me do this. However, I believe in this tagline of Nike, 'Just do it'.

I came up with an idea and gave it a go. I called my local WHSmith in Borehamwood, Hertfordshire, where I grew up. I spoke to the manager and explained I am an author and the local newspaper, the *Borehamwood & Elstree Times*, is writing an article about me, and I would love to get it into your store, where I can do a book signing and attract more customers. How would you feel about that? The manager was delighted and agreed to do it, and asked what dates would work, which I said I would get back to him on.

I then called the *Borehamwood & Elstree Times* and said, 'I am doing a book signing in WHSmith in Borehamwood and would they like to come, photograph it and put it in their paper'. Again, they agreed and asked when I am doing this signing event, and I said I'll get back to them. I then organised a date on a Saturday that worked for them both.

The book signing was hilarious. I was given this little table, I invited my friends and family to come and I sold about 17 books. After they left, I was sitting there watching the world go by. A lady approached me and said, 'Excuse me dear, where is the stationery section?' I replied, 'I don't work here, I am an author and am signing books'. I am certain J.K. Rowling never had this experience.

To make matters worse, I had to bear a loss of £12 that day. It happened when I left and went into the car park, with a parking ticket only valid for three hours, and I had to pay for the extra time.

The positive that did come out of it was I got my first edition into about 50 of the WHSmith travel stores, located in the airports and train stations. When my family and I travelled to Disney in Florida, I felt quite proud to have my book on the shelves at Gatwick Airport, London.

Figure 16.1

It may seem impressive that I managed to organise getting my book into WHSmith. The truth is that I just asked the question and like most things in sales, I just took action and did it.

Figure 16.2

17
Conducting a Meeting

'Some people want it to happen, some wish it would happen, others make it happen'.

—Michael Jordan

Having attended over 5000 meetings in my sales career to date, for both myself and in training for my clients, I've learned some incredible lessons in terms of both what to do and what not to do.

Let me start with 'what NOT to do, EVER AGAIN'. I recall my first few sales meetings where for the first five minutes I spoke to the prospect about the geographical area I looked after on the M4 corridor and the post-codes that covered and what my role as a sales executive entailed. Whilst I was boring the poor prospect to death, I was oblivious to a few key points:

This prospect did not have a single interest in the geographical areas I managed; I mean why would he?

I failed to give any value whatsoever.

I didn't engage the prospect at all and verbally threw up all over him.

I didn't deliver anything that would have been even the slightest bit beneficial to the prospect.

Apart from those points, it was an incredible introduction. So let me give you an example from the opposite side of the spectrum.

When you meet the prospect in the reception area and they walk you to their office, get them talking about themselves. Just ask anything that shows you're interested and gets them talking.

As a guideline, I suggest the following: 'I understand you've been here for X years'. (You'll get this information from their LinkedIn profile.) 'How did you get into the industry?'

Once you get into their office, depending on how open they are to talk on the walk to the office, pick up something about them in their office; for example, a picture of them playing golf, picture with their family, etc.

In a training session, my client made the fatal error of seeing the prospect was an Arsenal fan, and to build rapport, he lied and said he was a 'massive Gunners fan'. The prospect's eyes lit up at the thought that he could chat football with a fellow Gunner and asked, 'Where do you sit at the Emirates?', to which my client quickly lied and said, 'the west upper'. The prospect asked, 'Who Arsenal should play upfront for the coming game?', and at that point it was both obvious and painful to watch that my client had lied. There is a significant difference between showing an interest and lying; never cross that line. In the meeting, depending on the prospect's behaviour, it's wise to set an informal agenda.

So, after you have built rapport, and again the duration of this is dependent on the type of person you're in front of, lay out an informal agenda. I would suggest saying something along these lines: 'Thank you for inviting me in today. I'd like to set an informal agenda if I may to ensure you get exactly what you need out of the meeting to help you make an informed decision. Before I start, please tell me specifically what you'd like to get out of today's meeting?'

'I'd like to talk about companies that we have helped liked yours and the results we've helped them achieve. I want to get an understanding of both the challenges your sales team face and the aspirations you have for the business. At that point, I'll hopefully be in a position to make some recommendations of how I feel we can add most value'.

'Is there anything else you'd like to add to that?'

'Great, well, I have an hour to spend with you, does that work for you?'

You'll see, most of the work comes in the preparation and the follow-up, not the meeting itself. I compare it to a boxing match, you can spend months training and preparing for it and it's over in a matter of minutes, or seconds if you're caught out.

One of the things I recommend you discuss in the meeting is similar companies you've helped and most importantly what you helped them achieve. In order to prepare for this, you need to do your research and have a success story (aka case study) prepared to discuss. Please do not make the error of thinking that you're unable to discuss it because you haven't personally helped similar companies. If the company you represent has helped, then 'you' have helped. Your job is to find out exactly how and what was achieved. Never lie, you'll get caught and then your and your company's reputation will be tarnished.

At the end of every meeting, I follow the 'SAS (Summarise, Action, Steps)' process:

Summarise – This is why taking clear notes during the meeting is imperative. I spend around three to five minutes summarising the pertinent points that were discussed and end by asking, 'Have I missed anything?' This allows the prospect to add something.

Action – You must make the next steps crystal clear to the prospect in terms of what you're committing and what you want the prospect to commit too. This can be a variety of things depending on the sales cycle (length of time to secure the business), and can include the following:

- Get the prospect to invite other stakeholders involved in the decision-making process along for a second meeting.
- Set up a trial or demo of your product or service.
- Arrange to get some key information.
- Agree dates to get your proposal over and time frames to follow-up.

The point is to ensure both you and the prospect are aware of what is expected of them, so that things don't get held up.

Steps – To maintain control of the sales process, you must agree what the next steps are. This could be the date and time to be specific. If that's the case, confirm that in the room and get them to look at their calendar. This way, you can send a meeting invite then and there and they will be forced to accept the invite. This does not mean you can guarantee they will pick up your call; however, you can do the VET technique I mentioned earlier in this book, and the message will be, 'Hi NAME, it is Tony Morris here. I am just calling *as I promised*, you must be on the other line or engaged in a meeting. Please call me back on XXX and I'll try you again in an hour'. Now you are a professional following up, as opposed to a pest chasing them.

The follow-up is an area a lot of salespeople get wrong. They either don't follow up or do the same at the wrong time with the wrong message. As discussed earlier, it's imperative that when you finish a meeting, both parties are crystal clear on what is expected of one another. If this is done efficiently, then the follow-up is easy, as long as you remember to do it. It's vital that you utilise the CRM system that your company has, and if they don't have one, then you get one. I use HubSpot, as there is a basic license fee and it does exactly what my team and I need. It allows us to keep all notes about the prospect, enters the deals into a pipeline and organises all the call reminders, so you don't have to be bothered.

There was a study by the Institute of Sales Marketing Management (ISMM) that said 90% of salespeople quit by the third attempt and 90% of prospects buy between the fifth and twelfth attempts. Now this depends on the product or service you sell and the sales cycle. However, the point is: the top 1% salespeople are more successful than the other 99% because they do not quit at the third attempt.

18

Proposals

'Great things are done by a series of small things brought together'.

—Vincent van Gogh

I have been asked many times what the perfect proposal looks like. The answer is it all depends on what your prospect wants to see. There is no one size fits all. Your job is to create numerous templates that you can use to tailor a proposal that you feel will suit your prospect.

I am sharing one idea I did when I set up my sales training company in 2006. I called the top 10 competitors that I was aware of. I posed as a prospect and enquired about sales and sales management training. I did this for three reasons.

Firstly, it's always good to know what your competitors are doing and what they charge.

Secondly, I wanted to see if I could learn what to do or not to do, as the case may be over the phone. In terms of the questions they ask, I also noticed how they overcame my objections and how they tried to close.

Thirdly, and the reason I mention this idea, I got them all to send me a proposal to my Hotmail account. This allowed me to see the various templates they used and how they compiled their proposal, based on our detailed conversations. I took what I considered to be the best bits and amalgamated them into my own proposal. Again, I tailor each proposal based on the prospect's needs and behaviour, and this trick has proven very useful.

On one of these calls, I said to the training company that I have a few menswear shops in Moorgate, the City of London. I was enquiring about how much their management training costs. The person asked me a few questions about why I felt they needed training and what I saw as the biggest challenges they faced. I answered these in the best way I could, bearing in mind this was a made-up scenario. After listening to my response, he asked, 'What would the ideal result be, if I chose to put them through a training course?' I produced a couple of points such as an improvement in morale and being able to help their sales teams to cross-sell and upsell more effectively. He then asked my favourite question, 'What do you want to "invest" in your management team, to help them achieve those goals?'

Brilliant! He built the value of me doing it and I no longer saw it as a cost, I saw it as an investment. For the past 16 years, I never ask a prospect how much do they want to spend on training or what's their budget; it's always 'what do they want to "invest" to achieve a, b and c?'

These calls were extremely beneficial to me, and we do them every year, to see the changes they have made and what we can continue to learn.

To clarify, the reason why it's important to understand your prospect's behaviour before submitting your proposal is that different behaviours will be interested to see different things. A blue behaviour (analytical) will crave detail, particularly data. It goes without saying that you need to check the spelling, grammar and punctuation, as blue behaviours are much less forgiving of errors. We recently lost a deal because we wrote the following email a few days after sending our proposal:

Hi
Any further thoughts on my proposal?
Kind regards
Matt

When gaining feedback, the prospect felt it was very unprofessional that we didn't use his name at the beginning of the email. I happen to agree; however, my associate said it was a quick email sent when he was on a train. In my opinion, that associate missed the point here and should have realised a blue behaviour would have reacted terribly to this. I think deciding to not go ahead with us on this basis was extreme; however, it's a great lesson learned.

In my business, whenever we lose a deal, we get a colleague to call the prospect on the associate's behalf.

The reason for this is we feel only then will the prospect tell us the truth. If the prospect did not like us, they are unlikely to tell us, as it is confrontational and they are much more likely to say that our prices were too expensive, as that's an easier way out. I would recommend you do the same and these are the words I suggest:

'Hi, is that NAME? Hi NAME, it is Tony Morris here and I'm an associate with XXX. The reason for my call is I understand you met with my colleague Mike recently and decided to not move forward with him. At XXX, we strive for excellence, and we would really value your honest feedback on why you chose not to work with Mike. You will not offend me, we simply want to learn'.

And then you need to wrap up. Do not lead it and say, 'Was it our prices?', as this defeats the object.

My colleague did a call on my behalf a few years ago. The prospect said, 'Tony's proposal didn't have page numbers, and if he can miss that, what else would he miss while actually implementing it'.

I won't repeat the words I used when Mike shared this feedback with me; however, the point remains that it was important to the prospect and I got it wrong. I have never forgotten to insert page numbers on my proposals ever again.

19
Selling with NLP

'Life is 10% what happens to you and 90% how you react to it'.

—Lou Holtz

What Is NLP?

It's only been around since 1970 and seems to appear more and more in sales. Many people have different interpretations of what NLP is, but it's an understanding of the mind. Let's first look at what the words 'neuro linguistic programming' actually mean:

1. Neuro (brain)
2. Linguistic (language)
3. Programming (patterns)

The difference – why are some people competent and others exceptional at doing something?

Most exceptional people are unaware of what makes them special, and this is called unconscious competence – NLP makes you aware of why you are exceptional.

Richard Bandler and John Grinder created it in the 1970s, and they discovered that people have three basic methods of perceiving the world around them: visual, auditory and kinaesthetic (VAK).

Please answer these 15 questions in a VAK survey I got from Kerry Johnson's book *Selling with NLP*, and the answers to these will determine what your preferred method of communication is, as we all have one, even though we use all three.

Before taking the test myself, I knew I was a visual, I just didn't know it was labelled this way. I knew I was visual because whenever someone explains things to me, I automatically visualise it in my mind. If you ask me a question about my past, I will recollect some images of my past and would be able to recall specific details, such as the location, the colours, etc. Once I understood that I was a visual, it made me think back to when I was younger in school and how I revised for exams, and I was always better at learning diagrams and found biology an easy subject to study. I was able to absorb information and understand concepts much more effectively by seeing pictures or watching videos, as this was clearly my preferred method of communication.

So how powerful would it be to know how other people take information in and be able to communicate through their preferred method? Well, now you can with

NLP. Therefore, when you know someone is visual, you communicate visually. You show them tables, graphs, images that communicate your point. Therefore, if you're ever delivering a presentation, and there's an audience of more than five people, you need to have slides or use a flip chart to communicate to the visual learners. When you're speaking, you'll be communicating to the auditory learners and then you need to have something out, literature, a product or something that the kinaesthetic learners will touch and feel.

You are in control of your thoughts. You control your mind, state, internal representations, physiology, behaviour and outcomes. If you are going to have an attitude, you may as well have a positive one.

Preferred Modes of Thinking

Tick what appeals to you the most and you can tick more than one for each question:

1. A. I love to listen to music.
   B. I enjoy art galleries and window shopping.
   C. I feel compelled to dance to good music.
2. A. I would rather take an oral test than a written one.
   B. I was good at spelling in school.
   C. I tend to answer test questions using my 'gut' feeling.
3. A. I've been told that I have a great speaking voice.
   B. My confidence increases when I look good.
   C. I enjoy being touched.

4. A. I can resolve problems more quickly when I talk out loud.

   B. I would rather be shown an illustration than have something explained to me.

   C. I find myself holding or touching things as they are being explained.

5. A. I can usually determine sincerity by the sound of a person's voice.

   B. I find myself evaluating others based on their appearance.

   C. The way others shake hands with me means a lot.

6. A. I would rather listen to an audio book than read books.

   B. I like to watch TV and go the movies.

   C. I like hiking and other outdoor activities.

7. A. I can hear even the slightest noise that my car makes.

   B. It's important that my car is kept clean, inside and out.

   C. I like a car that feels good when I drive it.

8. A. Others tell me that I'm easy to talk to.

   B. I enjoy 'watching the people'.

   C. I tend to touch people when talking.

9. A. I am aware of what voices sound like on the phone, as well as face to face.

   B. I often remember what someone looked like, but not their name.

   C. I can't remember what people look like.

otery my

Selling with NLP

10. A. I often find myself humming or singing to the radio.
    B. I enjoy photography.
    C. I like to make things with my hand.
11. A. I would rather have an idea explained to me than read it.
    B. I enjoy speakers more if they have visual aids.
    C. I like to participate in activities rather than watch.
12. A. I am a good listener.
    B. I find myself evaluating others based on their appearance.
    C. I feel positive or negative towards others, sometimes without knowing why.
13. A. I can resolve problems more quickly when I talk out loud.
    B. I am good at finding my way using a map.
    C. I exercise because of the way I feel afterwards.
14. A. I like a house with rooms that allow for quiet areas.
    B. It's important that my house is clean and tidy.
    C. I like a house that feels comfortable.
15. A. I like to try to imitate the way people talk.
    B. I make a list of things I need to do each day.
    C. I've been told that I'm well-coordinated.

Now count them up and add up which you had more of. The answers are as follows:

A – Auditory
B – Visual
C – Kinaesthetic

227

Keep answers to yourself and see if your peers can identify your preferred method of communication.

How People Buy

We all have different ideas of reality – ways in which we perceive the world – and we can only really trust people who look at the world the way we do. If we feel understood, we give people our trust and open up more easily.

As the saying goes, 'If you can see the world through John Smith's eyes, you are in a stronger position to help John Smith buy from you'.

Selling to people the way they want to buy is the single most important element of every super seller's repertoire. People buy trust first, products second. If trust is present, clients are more receptive to suggestions and give more time to a salesperson.

A great example of this is the following scenario: three guys go on a camping weekend away. It's around 22:30 and they're sitting around a campfire and having chats. One of the guys is thinking to himself, 'This is so boring, and I would so much rather be at home with my partner'. The second guy is thinking to himself, 'I am so scared to go to sleep, as I am petrified if we hear foxes or other animals'. The third guy is thinking, 'I wish I were here with my girlfriend, as this would be romantic'. Exactly the same situation is seen through three different lenses.

NLP Epistemology – The Communication Model

We take things in through our five senses: visual, auditory, kinaesthetic (feelings), gustatory (taste) and olfactory (smell). We then use our beliefs and values to distort, delete, generalise and filter information.

I recall about eight years ago I bought a white M4. I chose white because it looked smart, and I rarely saw any white ones on the road. Within three weeks of it arriving, I saw about 30 white BMWs on the road. Those white BMWs were always there, I just deleted it from my brain when I saw them.

Internal Representation

When you hear something, how do you represent it in your mind? If I said, 'Imagine a cup of cappuccino', do you smell it, picture it or get a taste of it?

Your physiology will affect your internal representations. If you feel low, your body will be slumped, head down, and hence the saying, 'Keep your chin up'.

There are two clear ways of identifying someone's preferred method of communication, and this is what you can look for and listen out for in your meetings. The first thing is what words they use; in NLP they call it 'predicates'. I have put together a table of commonly used predicates for the three different senses, and as time goes on, you'll be able to see many more.

Predicates

VISUAL	AUDITORY	KINAESTHETIC
See	Imagined	Feel
Focus	Dramatic	Grab
Picture	Mind blowing	Handle
Vision	Hear	Grasp
Perception	Spell bound	Experienced
Clearly/clear	Listen	Excited
Perspective	Tell	Memorable
Sight	Resonate	Significant
Watching	Sounds like	Touch
Look	Express	Pressure
Bright	Ring	Know
Illustrate	Tone	Ambition
Highlight	Mention	Accomplishment
Reflect	Say	Epic
View	Ask	Rub
Show	Talk	Affect

The second way to identify a person's preferred method of communication is through their eye movements. There are many examples of this by the famous magician Derren Brown who is an NLP master practitioner that can be seen on YouTube. In NLP, they call these 'eye accessing cues' (Figure 19.1).

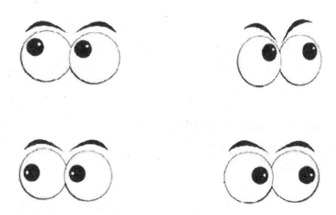

Figure 19.1

As you can see from this diagram, a visual person's eyes will always go up, and when they are recollecting an image from the past, their eyes will go up to the left. When they are creating a new image in the future, they will go up to the right. An auditory person's eyes go middle left when they are recalling a sound or a conversation, and middle right when they are creating a new sound. There is another sense called auditory digital (AD) where people's eyes go bottom left, and this is for people who do a lot of 'self-talk'.

Figure 19.2

A kinaesthetic person's eyes will always go bottom right when they are recalling their feelings, hence the saying, 'You look downright angry'.

Some good exercises to practise these techniques before going into a meeting are as follows:

Ask your friend/partner to talk for three minutes about things such as:

- The town in which they grew up.
- Their family members.
- Last vacation.

One person should notice the predicates they use and jot them down. Then ask for about one minute about how they picture the object or the situation.

1. What sounds do they remember?
2. What feelings came to mind?

Notice the predicates, and after a couple of minutes, ask which of the three did you remember best?

Eye Movements Exercise

Ask a colleague to describe their dream home and watch their eye movements. As they are creating an image, their eyes will either go:

Up right (visual)
Side right (auditory)
Down right (kinaesthetic)

Then ask them the first house they remember; their eyes should go in opposite direction as they are recalling a memory.

Ask someone leading questions using visual predicates. Enquire about the past.

What was the look on your wife's face when you proposed? Where do you see yourself in the business in the next five years? What will your dream house look like?

Selling to Visual Learners

Use the same words they use. When visuals hear words like 'show', 'clear', 'bright', 'perspective', 'picture' and 'view', they understand you more quickly because they don't have to take those extra moments to translate what you are saying into images. By talking in someone's preferred method, you are building rapport, because you are communicating that you understand this person. The fact that it is all happening at an unconscious level makes it more effective.

Selling property – 'Can't you just picture your family all sitting in this lovely dining room? I bet you can see how all this furniture will look when we fill this room up'.

At the beginning of a meeting – 'What do you see yourself accomplishing as a result of being with me today?'

Before a meeting, the director said to me, 'I'd like to see what you could offer me. I'd like you to give me a picture of how you would deliver the training. I have seen a few training companies for my team, but I'd like to get your perspective on how you would handle my team'.

For visuals, always keep brochures, graphs and pictures handy when selling to them. Any concept will be much more quickly understood if you can show a bar chart or a graph while you speak. A good close to a visual is 'Do you like what you see?'

Visual people speak very quickly, breathe fast and high in the chest, and their voices tend to be slightly higher in pitch.

Selling to Auditory Learners

'How does this sound so far?'

If you are selling a car, point out how smoothly the engine runs.

Music being played in shops has a huge impact on buyers. In a study at Loyola University, it was found that when the music was slow in supermarkets, sales were 38.2% higher than when fast music was played. When shoppers were asked what they thought about the music, 33% didn't know what kind had been played, and 39% denied there was any music at all. The music did its work on an unconscious level.

Selling to Kinaesthetic Learners

'How do you feel about this?'
'How does this grab you so far?'

'What's your impression on these unique features?'

'What do you feel you would like to accomplish as a result of our meeting today?'

Give kinaesthetic things to touch, they will buy five times faster. For example, when selling a car, touch the seats, the gearbox, dashboard controls, etc.

Selling to a Group

You want to mix all the predicates to keep everyone involved. If someone asks you to clarify something, answer by saying:

'Does this sound good so far?'

'If anyone can't get a handle on this so far, please raise your hand' (kinaesthetic).

Any presentation should include all three things to make it more enjoyable and stimulating to an audience. In Kerry Johnson's book, *Selling with NLP*, he claimed that the split between people's preferred method of communication is as follows:

Visual – 40%
Auditory – 30%
Kinaesthetic – 30%

A good example of mixing these up – a wife wants to be loved and she's an auditory person. The hubby is a kinaesthetic person and buys her chocolates and flowers. But the wife just wants to *hear* she is loved.

One of the best mismatches of predicates was in the first *Ghostbusters* movie. They are walking through a library, and Dan stops and says, 'Listen, did you smell that?'

When you next read the newspapers, magazines, an article or an email from your boss, try and look out for examples of the predicates that are used. Some great real-life examples from famous people I have heard and seen in the past are as follows.

Visual

David Beckham was interviewed and they asked him, 'You have one of the most precise passes in the game, how do you do it? What goes through your mind before you make that pass?' He replies, 'I see the pass pattern in my head. I see the player going into that space and I place an X in the middle of my mental playing field and I pass to the X that I see in my mind'.

Visuals are much better with faces than with names. They are good spellers, as they picture the entire word as they spell it out.

Auditory

Jimmy Connors (tennis player) – 'I listen to the way the ball sounds as it comes off the server's racket'.

Kinaesthetic

Bill Clinton is kinaesthetic. In his speeches, he talks a lot about caring and feelings. After his inauguration, he spent hours waiting to hug and shake hands with the hundreds of well-wishers.

Albert Einstein was a kinaesthetic. In interviews, his eyes always went down to the right. He came up with the theory of relativity imagining what it might feel like to ride a beam of light through the universe.

Are you the sort of person who goes around the office patting people on the back, rubbing shoulders?

Kinaesthetic people make frequent pauses in their conversations, as they are trying to access a feeling. They think to themselves, 'How do I feel about what he just asked me?'

Kinaesthetic people love to touch people and things. When you are talking to them across a desk, they are often playing with small objects they pick up without thinking about it, pens, paper clips, etc.

The uses of mental maps or representational systems are subconscious, and it's a way of organising all the stimuli we receive. If you know how to 'read' someone's mental map, you have a very powerful tool to use in understanding how someone's mind works.

20
Handle the Person, Not the Objection

'Don't be content with being average, average is as close to the bottom as it is to the top'.

—Richard Denny

When it comes to objections, there are two situations that you will face: a condition and an objection, these are very different.

Conditions – a situation out of your control where you cannot do anything, such as the has been made bankrupt, or just signed a contract with another company (if that contract covers every product/service that you offer).

Objections – these are something you can change and overcome.

Why Do You Think People Object?

Have you ever been into a shop where an annoying salesperson approaches you within a millisecond, wanting to know if they can help you? Usually you respond, 'I am just looking, thanks'.

As you look around, you feel the salesperson's eyes on you, making you feel uncomfortable and on edge. You are holding the item and the salesperson approaches you and asks, 'Would you like to try it on?' I call this 'commission breath' and no one likes it.

To avoid any confrontation, I normally put it over their till and say, 'I am just going to get my friend to get their opinion, and I'll be back,' and then never return to that shop again.

I lied to avoid an awkward situation or conversation. So it's fair to assume prospective customers may lie as well, which we take as an objection and give up.

Sometimes people object as they do not understand what it is that we are offering. Rather than saying to us, 'Can you be clearer with what you are offering?' Their quick response is, 'I am not interested' or 'I don't need that, thanks'.

It is important that we do not fear objections. We must accept them. We must not panic, and we must rise to the challenge. We must remember that we are not going to win on every occasion, but as long as we give it everything, it is a job done well.

What Do We Do if the Client Has an Objection?

The key is to listen and be calm. Many salespeople hear an objection (e.g., too expensive) and jump in without thinking, saying, 'We can match that price'. However, if they'd stayed calm, they may not have needed to throw a percentage of their commission and profits away.

If possible, it's good to relate to the client. 'Other people I have spoken to say that same thing, but what they have decided to do is. . .'.

The most important thing when handling the person is to listen, do not interrupt. You must ask open-ended questions, as these will help you establish the facts. This will come with practice and confidence; however, it's important not to hesitate. You will not sound convincing and the client wants to trust you, so you must say it with belief and conviction.

You must be clear and to the point, don't be scared to pause occasionally so that the client can digest the information. Use your voice to highlight key areas.

Remember, some objections are buying signals, as it shows the prospect is interested, so you should welcome them as an opportunity to sell, rather than feel a sense of rejection. Don't panic, just smile, and say to yourself, I can handle this; I know I will make a sale. If the prospect says, for example, 'Your contracts are too long', that is a buying signal, as you could reframe this by saying, If my contract was shorter the prospect would buy.

In some situations, you will have to sell to an influencer and there is nothing that can be done to avoid this.

You can say, 'I am an expert at what I do, and you are an expert at what you do, doesn't it make sense that I am there in the final meeting when you discuss productivity and profitability, so I can give you all the right answers to make an informed decision for the business? What I don't want to happen is that they ask you questions that you can't answer, which will affect the decision they make'.

Here is a list of objections that my clients get and the rebuttals they use to overcome their objections.

Market Is Not Good at the Moment (Property)

This is known as an emotional objection, as it's based on an opinion. The best way to deal with an objection like this is to use a technique called 'a third party proof', where you relate it to yourself or a client of yours. It shows empathy with the prospect and aims to put them at ease.

'I am surprised to hear that. Can I ask, what are you basing that on? I do understand how you feel; many of my clients have felt the same. They have found with our company that it's the best possible time to invest their money and take advantage of the market condition'.

You can use this technique for when a client has heard bad things about your company or has had a bad experience like the following.

Bad Experience

ME: I am sorry to hear that, what happened?

PROSPECT: We used your company in the past but found the after-sales support was poor, and they never got back to us.

I do understand how you feel; many of my clients have felt exactly the same way. But what they have now found is that our after-sales support team has been through lots of training and we now pride ourselves on delivering exceptional levels of service. I would like to demonstrate to you that we can fulfil your requirements and ensure no more mistakes. When can we meet to discuss this?

Where possible, it's essential to isolate an objection. You also need to know if this is the only objection the prospect has, and if so, can we deal with it?

A good example of this is a letting agent I trained:

TENANT: I think the property needs a lick of paint as it's looking very tired.

NEGOTIATOR: Is that the only thing stopping you from making an offer for the property?

TENANT: Yes.

NEGOTIATOR: I know the landlord very well. If I can get him to agree to give this property a lick of paint, will you make an offer today?

These two techniques will ensure that there are no more objections to come and you have then preclosed the tenant to gain his commitment.

Need to Speak to My Partner

I mentioned earlier that sometimes you will have to sell to an influencer who then gives you the objection, 'I need to speak to my partner or my boss'. Who is now selling your products/services?

He is, and he's not as good as you because you are the sales professional. Your objective here is to make sure that he is in the best position to sell your offering in the best light possible.

There are three parts to this rebuttal, which I would handle as follows.

Firstly, you want to make sure that he is not going to discuss it with his boss, instead he's going to recommend you to his boss. 'I appreciate that you need to speak to your boss, but putting him/her to one side, if it was just down to you, would you go ahead? If yes, great. To ensure I haven't missed anything, the reason you want to invest in Project X with us is that it has a three-year rental guarantee; it's in the centre of city, so it will be always in demand; and it has the best view in the block'.

'What can I send you that your boss will want to see?'

'When, realistically, will you be speaking with your boss? . . . Lovely, I will call you on Wednesday to gain your valued feedback. What time do you prefer, morning or afternoon?'

You can now attempt a trial close by saying, 'If your boss is as comfortable as you are when we speak on Wednesday, will you be in a position to move things forward?'

I Am Happy with My Current Supplier

One objection you may get when cold calling is, 'I am happy with my current supplier'. The key to creating an opportunity here is to try and identify one area that could be improved and make that problem worse in the prospect's mind. Then you are in with a chance.

Here is an example of this with one of my clients in the waste management industry.

SALESPERSON: I understand that, and who are you currently working with?

PROSPECT: X.

SALESPERSON: What products/service do you get with them?

PROSPECT: General waste and glass recycling.

SALESPERSON: How do you find working with them?

PROSPECT: Yes, not bad at all.

SALESPERSON: What areas do you feel they could improve?

Many salespeople ask 'Are you happy with them?' and when the prospect responds 'Yes' they are immediately on the back foot.

Another way of asking this question is 'On a scale of 1–10, 10 being exceptional service and being awful, where would you rate? What's required to make it a 10?'

PROSPECT: I think they are pretty good, but I guess they could always be slightly cheaper, and I don't have much contact with my account manager.

SALESPERSON: Can I ask why you would prefer to have more regular contact?

PROSPECT: I guess I would have the peace of mind that we are using the right service and paying the right price.

SALESPERSON: I appreciate that you are sharing that with me, and one of the many reasons our clients work with us is because they are allocated a dedicated consultant. We have a monthly review to ensure that they are happy with everything and they are paying the right price. From what you've kindly shared, I would recommend us meeting, so I can find out more about the recycling processes you have, and discuss how we can add value. I am currently available on Tuesday and Thursday next week, which is best for you?

This is an ideal scenario, and the prospect won't always share an area or two that he feels could be improved. Not all is lost, as there are more ways to create opportunities:

SALESPERSON: What are you not getting that you'd like?

PROSPECT: I am quite happy and you know what they say, if it ain't broke, don't fix it.

SALESPERSON: I do appreciate that but if you were even considering looking elsewhere what one thing would you change?

PROSPECT: Honestly, I can't think of anything.

SALESPERSON: It sounds like you clearly have a very good set up with XXX. If they couldn't offer a service you required, who would you then look at?

PROSPECT: I am not sure, it's not happened.

SALESPERSON: It's not happened yet, but it might, and I want us to be your backup supplier in case of any eventuality. I suggest having a meeting so you are comfortable with me and my company if we are ever needed as a backup. I am currently available on Tuesday and Thursday next week, which day is best for you?

Imagine they have a backup supplier and say, 'If we ever have an emergency, they already have someone in place'. Worry not; all is not lost, read on for the next bite at the cherry:

SALESPERSON: In the five years of working with XXX, when did you last review to ensure you are getting the best level of service and at best price?

PROSPECT: We haven't really, as we did not feel it was needed.

SALESPERSON: I appreciate that. As I am sure you are aware, there have been some dramatic changes in the waste management industry in the past few years, and I would recommend meeting me so that you can benchmark alongside us, and ensure that you have the right products and services at the right price. I am currently available on Tuesday and Thursday next week, which is best for you?

Whenever you find a prospect that has a supplier in place, with whom they claim to be happy, remind yourself to ask the following questions.

Feedback
'How do you find working with XXX? What areas do you feel they could improve?

If there was one thing that would make you even consider looking elsewhere, what would it be?'

Review
'In the past five years you've been with, when did you last review to ensure you're getting the best service and paying the right price?'

Backup
'If XXX let you down or couldn't offer you a product you needed, whom would you look at?'

Your Product Is too Expensive

One objection that will always arise is around money, and there are ways to deal with it rather than agree to match the lower price to get the business. Is a Porsche more expensive than a Skoda? One is very different from the other, and, clearly, it's not apples for apples.

SALESPERSON: That's interesting feedback; can I ask, what are you comparing us to?

PROSPECT: Your training is costing £1500 per day and I have looked at another trainer who costs £1100 per day.

SALESPERSON: That's fine. Can I ask, if our prices were the same, who would you choose?

If they say, 'your competitor', you've lost badly, go home, think about it and move on.

However, if they say, 'you', say, 'I am pleased to hear that and why would you choose me?'

Now, let the prospect sell you back to you. This is one of the most effective ways to influence and persuade someone, as they won't argue with themselves.

Once you know what you are being compared to, you can then build the value and only focus on the difference, which makes it easier for the prospect to justify it in their mind.

Send Me Information

This is normally a fob off and a polite way of saying, 'I don't want to discuss this any further'. Remind yourself that the objective of your call is to arrange a meeting, and literature is not going to help you achieve that.

ME: Our literature is very generic; it will be far more beneficial for us to meet so that I can explain exactly how we have helped companies like yours. I am currently available on Tuesday and Thursday next week, which is best for you?

Depending on the rapport you build with the prospect, you can say the following:

ME: We both know you are not going to read the literature. It will be far more beneficial for us to meet so that I can give you an idea of the savings we could offer you and how we can improve your service. I am available on Tuesday or Thursday, which day is best for you?

If the prospect becomes adamant that he needs to see something first, agree to send it and close by saying the following:

ME: Okay, what specifically do you want to see?

Fine, I will send that out to you, and once you have digested it, naturally you will have questions to ask, which I can answer in our meeting. I am available on Tuesday or Thursday, which day is best for you?

Your Competitor, Who Is Very Similar to You, Is Cheaper

This is an objection a big hotel group I train gets on a regular basis.

HOTEL: There's always a difference between hotels.
PROSPECT: For this brand, it really is a very sim-
            ilar offer.
HOTEL: If we were priced the same, who would
            you choose?

If they say 'your competitor' then you are screwed, and I have no ideas for you, except to see if that hotel group has any jobs available for you.

If they say yes, however, you say, 'I am pleased to hear that and why would you choose me?' Now, let the prospect sell you back to you.

My recommendation is to brainstorm with your sales teams the typical objections you all get, write them all down and discuss the rebuttals that have worked the best for all the different objections. This is not cheating. This is being better prepared than your competition.

21
Positive Words and Language

'Opportunity does not knock, it presents itself when you beat down the door'.

—Kyle Chandler

You can use all the best sales techniques in the world, but if you come across like a negative teenager on the phone with poor vocabulary and negative words, you are doomed to fail.

People like to talk to positive people, and along with sounding enthusiastic, passionate and genuine, you need to make sure the words you use have a positive impact on your prospects and client base. In the following table, see if you can think of the positive alternatives to the words provided in the left column.

Sorry to keep you waiting
I'm afraid/unfortunately
But
I hope/I think
Don't worry
No problem/no worries
Bear with me
I'm sorry
Don't hesitate to call
Pop in (for a quick chat)
Is it convenient to speak?

The key is to use positive language in every conversation and in your every email correspondence. It will take practice in the beginning, and after some time it becomes part of your daily vocabulary. In the following table, check these positive alternatives to the words mentioned in the previous table:

Sorry to keep you waiting	Thank you for waiting
I'm afraid/unfortunately	At present/since
But	However/having said
I hope/I think	I'm sure/I trust
Don't worry	Be assured that
No problem/no worries	Certainly/my
Bear with me	Just a moment
I'm sorry	I do apologise
Don't hesitate to call	Please feel free to call
Pop in (for a quick chat)	Arrange to meet with
Is it convenient to speak?	Thanks for taking my call

If, like me, you work in a variety of industries, it's imperative to understand the terminology that they use and build up a dictionary for every industry. This will build your credibility and demonstrate your expertise and knowledge of their market. Here are just a few examples of the words I use when speaking to people from different industries in which I work.

Estate Agents
Salesmen – negotiators
  Customers – tenants, landlords, applicants
  Meeting – viewings/valuations

Recruitment
Salesmen – recruitment consultants
  Prospecting – headhunting

IT Software
Salesmen – consultants
  Industry – vertical
  Meeting – sit
  Current supplier – incumbent supplier

In addition to the words we use, there are clever techniques to influence people's thoughts.

If I say, 'Do not think of a blue elephant roller skating in a supermarket.'

Your brain must think about the blue elephant, in order to avoid thinking about it. These embedded commands can be used for worthwhile causes in your sales pitch like this:

I work with many UK and overseas property investment companies. To get an investor to focus on two
areas in one go, you can use an embedded command
such as: 'Don't think about the returns this investment
will make, think about the long-term security for your
family'.

When I discuss sales training with my prospects,
I embed commands such as: 'Don't think about the
increase to your bottom line, think about the improvement to your team's morale'.

When I come across a prospect that already has a
training company in place, I often embed this command:
'Don't think of the negative points of your current training provider, think of the benefits we can bring you'.

Imagine what you would like your prospects to think
about and work out embedded commands to get across
in your pitch.

I discussed earlier about selling with NLP. Language
is an integral part of this. Reframing and using meta-
phors are very powerful ways to deliver a concept.

Reframing is putting any concept or situation into a
different perspective. Take something that is negative
or neutral and turn it into something positive. Imagine
reframing a picture, what a difference it can make.

If you ask someone, 'How are you?' It gets an automatic response. Even if the person is feeling like crap,
they'll still respond, 'Fine, thanks, how are you?'

Reframe it to 'How has your morning been so far?'

When they have to think about what you've said, it
translates into caring, which translates into greater rapport
and trust.

At the end of a training session, I always ask my delegates, 'What have you learned today?' This gets them to think of what they have learned and taken away. If I ask 'Did you have a good day?', they have less to think about and the answers will be less informative.

Another question I ask after covering a session on overcoming nerves when presenting is 'How do you feel differently now?' This presupposes you will feel differently now and gets my delegates to focus on the difference.

Mary Kay Cosmetics has reframed their salespeople. Instead of calling them 'cosmetics salespeople', they are now referred to as 'Mary Kay Consultants' – this conveys the idea that this person will help solve problems.

Metaphor – when describing something, try to link it to you listeners' experience. For example, while talking to your PA, describe a great sale you made by comparing it to a wonderful job he or she did for you.

In NLP, a metaphor is any figure of speech or story that gets your listeners to identify themselves with your ideas. If I spoke about my training I could say, 'The difference between me and other trainers is like the difference between a Porsche and a Volkswagen. One helps you enjoy the ride while getting you there, the other just gets you there'.

An insurance broker was asked by a carpet manufacturer what the difference was between 'whole-life insurance' and 'term insurance'. He answered, 'The difference between whole-life insurance and term insurance is like the difference between indoor and outdoor carpeting.

Both look nice, but one lasts a whole lot longer and gives you more benefits in the end'.

I would recommend brainstorming with your fellow sales team the words that you should use on a daily basis.

Here are just some of the positive words I use in my daily vocabulary:

Specialists	High quality	Calibre
Highly recommended	Unique	Positive
Valued	Committed	Driven
Value for money	Tailored	Bespoke
Cost effective	Flexible	Peace of mind
Priority	Transparent	Preferred
Motivated	Successful	Pride
Professional	Expertise	Ownership
Reassurance	Competitive	Affordable
Imperative	Passionate	Motivated
Well established	Reputable	Experience
Knowledgeable	Enthusiastic	Paramount
Accountable	Flexible	Dedicated

The key thing to remember is 'facts tell, stories sell'. Therefore, along with having the right language, you need to be able to have the right stories to illustrate key messages. People will always remember the story, not the key facts. Create a story deck with your sales team, so that when something arises, you can choose the appropriate story to tell.

22
Lead Generation

'Things do not happen. Things are made to happen'.
—John F. Kennedy

Some companies you work for will provide you with a fantastic database that has loads of qualified leads ready to receive your sales call. Other companies won't have anything, and in sales it is best to expect the unexpected.

The first thing to start is to get an understanding of the company's target market. These are some questions you should be asking your boss:

- Which industries are their typical clients with whom they have been successful?
- Have they got a database of old and inactive clients that you could start canvassing?
- Have they got a database of prospects that the previous salespeople have not converted for whatever reason?

- Have they got a database of every client they have ever done work with, which may not have been called of late to try and generate new business or cross-sell or upsell?

Once you have got your answers for these questions, try some of the following proven ways of generating new leads.

Referrals – ask every client who could they recommend that could benefit from your products/services. Ask your boss if you are allowed to offer them a bottle of wine or a percentage of their next invoice in return. Later in this book, I will share some great strategies of exactly how to ask for referrals.

I remember, I had just finished delivering training at Jurys Inn's hotels. They are a group of 38 independent hotels across the UK and Ireland. At the end of the training, the sales team was absolutely buzzing and could not wait to put into practice what they had learned. The sales director, Marc Webster, thanked me and said, 'It was even better than I had hoped for'. I said, 'I am so pleased to hear that and you have a great sales team, and you have clearly done a fantastic job managing them'. I then said, 'I know you have been in the hotel industry for many years and I imagine you're very well connected. Who do you know that would benefit from my sales training?' He went quiet and was thinking, and then after about 20 seconds said, 'I would be more than happy to recommend you, because you have been exceptional, but I just can't think of anyone, I'm so sorry'. I said, 'No need to apologise at all, and if you do think of anyone, let me know'. And then we sat and just had some chit-chat. And suddenly it then struck me that the mug I was drinking from was branded Jurys Inn, as were the coasters, the pads and pens. I said, 'Marc, which company do you get your branded merchandise from?' He said, 'Dukes of London, why do you ask?' I said, 'They would be an ideal company for me. Would you be so kind to introduce me to them?' Without even replying he got out his mobile and made a call. He said, 'Andy, the sales director, is a mate of mine, he'll love you'. Marc left Andy a voice mail and said he'll do an introduction for me.

Two weeks later, I was meeting Andy at his offices in Old Street. Three weeks later, I was delivering sales training to Andy's team at Dukes of London.

So, if your clients cannot think of someone to refer you, help them. Ask about the suppliers they work with, as they might be your next whale.

Dissect your biggest clients if possible – for example, Rolls Royce has so many parts in terms of suppliers and subsidiaries, so dissect and explore.

Ask your clients for the recommendation from their previous place of work. Whom could they recommend speaking to there?

Contact the direct competitors of your clients – in a meeting, ask the prospective customer about their competitors in business; these can be your next leads. Do that in every meeting.

Introduce lucrative schemes to your clients – I offer my clients £50 for an introduction (not a referral) and a further £100 if any business is generated from it. We run email campaigns to all the clients offering them this scheme and it generates many warm leads.

Look at your clients' testimonials – call them, saying, 'We also work with XXX'. Use this as your introduction.

Use LinkedIn – look up to your competitor, see who they're connected with, and call them.

Every industry is part of an association. I used to spend days cold calling promotional merchandise companies and would try and make meetings with the sales director or MD. While spending hours to get hold of the right person, when I did, they just said they only have a small sales team and didn't want to invest thousands of pounds on such a small team. After a little bit of research, I found out that most promotional merchandise companies were members of the British Promotional Merchandise Association (BPMA). It took me two calls to get hold of Gordon Glenister, the director general of BPMA and arrange a meeting at their head office in Islington, London. In the meeting, Gordon explained they had about 800 members that are made up of individual promotional merchandising companies. Once Gordon saw the value and benefits I can bring to his members, he endorsed my training, and designed and circulated emails to all 800 of them. This opened the door to a new industry for me and very quickly introduced me to many new clients. We ran monthly training workshops for his members, and within six months, five of the companies had booked me for some bespoke training, as they had large sales teams.

Go as a visitor to exhibitions – look at the big exhibition halls such as National Exhibition Centre (NEC) in Birmingham, Earl's Court and Olympia in London and G-Mex in Manchester, and look at the calendars to decide which ones are relevant to you in terms of having the right sort of business. You can attend for free and pick up many leads, along with potentially meeting the decision-makers that you need to be targeting.

Networking clubs – look at the possibility of clubs such as BNI, for networking. Attend the business growth show or any other free networking events that are available and will have companies that require your products/services.

Speak to your friends – I know it's obvious, but how many of you have genuinely asked all your friends and their parents for leads (people know people who know other people)?

Lead Generation Ideas If You Work in Recruitment

The day after leaving Capscan, which was my first B2B sales role, the recruitment consultant who had placed me at Capscan called me to wish me luck on my next job and then asked where I was going. I explained I was going to try my luck as a trader, and his enthusiasm disappeared. I realised he didn't call me to wish me all the best, but to find out if there was a sales opportunity at my new place.

Do you do this?

If you're in recruitment, I think this is an extremely smart way of getting continuous leads. You simply connect with every candidate you place on LI and the second you get alerted from LI that they're moving on, you call to congratulate them and then find out where they're going and the name of their boss. In addition, you now have an opportunity to replace that person at the company, which hopefully is still your client.

Every time you interview a candidate, ask them other companies at which they have interviewed. You now know those companies are recruiting and now you have a great prospect.

Once you are calling and checking the candidate's references, you can see if that company is a potential fit for your business.

Pipeline

As you start attending meetings and sending out quotes, you are now building up your pipeline of business. Some companies you work for will have a great customer relationship management (CRM) tool, and you will be able to track and monitor your pipeline very easily, but some will not. On the following page is a traffic light pipeline spreadsheet I created, where I enter every deal I am working on, and whether I met with them or just sent

Hot	£	Warm	£	Cold	£
IBM	£10,000	ABC	£4560	STU	£453
HP	£17,000	DEF	£3210	VWX	£45
ABC	£4,500	GHI	£3879	YZ	£89
		JKL	£6540		
		MNO	£4559		
		PQR	£3000		
	£31,500		£25,748		

them a proposal without meeting them. This enables me to stay on top of every single deal and help me forecast when which business will be dropping in.

As part of a sales team, you will probably have weekly or monthly sales meetings, where your sales manager or director will ask, 'What have you forecast to drop this month?' This traffic light pipeline will help you calculate this out at the click of a button; it's the 'E'-shaped button in excel called 'sigma' which calculates every deal in a column. I have split the pipeline into three colours.

- Green is cold, which I define as 1 in 33% probability.
- Yellow is warm, which has 34–75% probability.
- Red is hot, which I have classed as 76–100% probability.

As an example, I may attend a meeting with an influencer. They are looking at five of my competitors and then they will be shortlisting two of us, who will present to the board of directors for a decision.

Once I have quoted, I would enter this company and the amount I proposed in green. Once I have gained positive feedback that we have been shortlisted, I would move them to yellow. Finally, when I get the go-ahead or have a better feeling about them, I would move them to red.

This pipeline is constantly moving and having companies added and omitted from it all the time. It's become my Bible now, as I can see in a snapshot all the deals on which I am working.

23
Gaining Referrals

'Champions keep playing until they get it right'.
—Billie Jean King

One of the most effective ways of doing business is by referral. Once you have done a great job for someone's business and they have personally recommended you to one of their friends or contacts, you are 90% on the way to sealing the deal by the time you first speak to them. It eliminates all the fear of dealing with you for the first time and questioning whether your product or service works. Whenever you can gain a referral, make sure you get one, as this will increase the amount of business you do over time.

Clients I work with who deal with many inbound enquiries always take the prospect's contact details and then ask how they heard about them. This a great way of understanding where your enquiries are coming from, so you can amend your marketing spend accordingly.

I do feel there is a better way of asking the question. The key is to create the perception that the majority of your business comes from referrals, as this gives the prospect the confidence that you are clearly good at what you do. For any inbound enquiry, I would suggest asking, 'Who recommended you to us?' You need to get all the sales team asking this question consistently, as this gives the perception that most of your business comes from recommendations.

I shared this idea with a property client who sells distressed properties. The directors and the sales team liked the idea so much that they changed the strapline on their business cards to 'By Referral Only'. This, along with many other ideas I will share with you later on in this chapter, increased their referral business by 37%.

Who says you can only gain a referral from your customers? What about the hundreds of prospects you speak to on a daily basis that, for whatever reason, you cannot help?

I was talking to the MD of a courier company the other day and after about a good 15-minute conversation it was clear that he didn't have a genuine need for my sales training. He only had two sales consultants, both of whom have been working with him for 40 years and planned on retiring soon. When they did, it will be the right time to speak to him.

ME: Mark, it has been an absolute pleasure in talking to you today, and clearly you have a very successful business. You must have some clients which have a sales team that could really benefit from the type of sales training we have been discussing?

He reeled off two companies off the top of his head, with the MD's name and phone number that he knew their sales team suffered and required my help.

I am pleased to say one of them became my client. I have already delivered six days' training for them and made an enormous difference. The other is in my pipeline, and they are reviewing the marketplace.

Sometime I think, Would Mark have recommended these two companies, if I hadn't asked? Probably not, and it's not because he's a horrible person or didn't want my business to succeed, it's just it wasn't on his radar. My job was to make him think about it and give me a name and a number. If possible, ask him to speak to the two people first, to give them a heads up that I will be calling.

A friend of mine significantly improved his qualified leads by carrying a printed letter of introduction for his clients to insert the name of the referral and sign. The easier you make it for your clients, the more likely they are to provide you with a referral. Here is an example of the letter he wrote:

I remember when I took my first mortgage at the age of 23. The broker, James, came over to my parents' house an evening to go through all the paperwork. We must have spent about two hours together, filling in countless forms and working out the best mortgage around my needs.

At the end of the evening, James turned round and said, 'Tony, I imagine that most of your friends have moved out or are looking to move out?'

I said, 'Absolutely and funny enough, four of us are all looking at the same block of flats'.

He said, 'How have you found dealing with me in finding you the right mortgage?'

Without hesitation I replied, 'You have been great, very friendly and extremely helpful'.

He asked me if I would recommend any of my friends in a similar situation to myself for him to talk to.

Without even thinking about it, I took out my mobile and gave him seven names and numbers to call that were all looking to move out into their first home, and would therefore require a mortgage.

I know I would never have given him my mates' numbers out of hand, as it wasn't something that even crossed my mind, but given the fact he was great to deal with and he asked for them, I obliged.

How many times have you done a great job and not asked for a referral? If you don't ask, you don't receive.

I know I was very guilty of this and felt sick at how much business I have let pass me by not asking that simple question.

Do not worry. As long as you do it now, every time, you will quickly catch up with yourself. You can always go back to some of your older clients and ask them.

I used to belong to a business networking club called Business Network International (BNI). This was set up to help companies get more business by referral. BNI is an extremely successful business and has been going for many years now.

They say every person knows 1000 people. When I first heard that I remember thinking, 'I've only got about five mates and three people in my family, so that's garbage'. But then I gave it a second thought and realised that I had over three clients, 600 connections on LinkedIn and approximately 200 friends on Facebook. Then I thought about all my parents' friends I knew, and the businesses they are involved in. The whole motto of BNI is 'givers gain', which means 'If I give you business, you are more likely to give me business'.

The same applies to gaining referrals. If you refer business to someone, they feel compelled to return the favour. Another great way of getting referrals is saying to your client, 'I meet many business contacts on a daily basis, so I can refer people to you. Who would be the ideal prospect for you?'

Get them to spell out for you the perfect contact for them. For example, for my courier clients it would be a warehouse manager, whereas for my business it would be a sales director or MD, depending on the size of the company.

When prospecting, it's worth targeting businesses that you want to work with, as well as businesses that may have clients you wish to work with. For example, I work very closely with a furniture company that specialises in furnishing 'buy to let' properties, and they work with approximately 65% of the UK estate agency market.

Estate agents are a great market for me, as I have trained about 45 agents all over the UK and achieved some incredible results for them. When I chose this particular furniture company to target, it took me about a year and a half of persistently cold calling them until I arranged a meeting. Since then, I have been able to refer them to some of my estate agency clients, and they have kindly returned the favour.

One idea that works very well is sending a handwritten card to every new client you work with. We have had some sales doctor–branded cards designed, and we send them out after training, thanking them for their business. In the card, we state that we work with many clients and would happily recommend them to any that they could benefit from. We ask them to email or call us to tell us who would be an ideal referral for them, and we make sure we chase them up to get this information. We aren't always able to refer people, but they are receptive when we ask for a referral in return.

Some of our clients have used this card idea for getting their name out there, which in turn has resulted in more referrals. Many estate agents we train send out a 'congratulations' card once the tenant has moved into their property. Some of my clients send out birthday cards or anniversary cards to their tenants. Imagine if a friend of theirs asks, 'I don't suppose you know any good agents around here that you could recommend, do you?' Who do you think is the first estate agent that springs to mind?

There are different ways of asking for a referral, and it all depends on what you are comfortable with, and on the relationship with your client.

If you have a very good, friendly relationship with your client:

CLIENT: If your mates walked into the pub, would you introduce me?
TENANT: Yes.
CLIENT: Great. Do me a favour. Take out your mobile and give me three names and numbers of contacts you feel could benefit from what I do.

Asking a client for a referral sometimes isn't enough for them, as they might find it hard to refer you, not knowing exactly what you look for in a lead.

I recently asked my waste management client for a referral, and she said, 'I'd love to help, but I don't know any companies with a sales team'. Fortunately, I had already spotted an opportunity, so I said to her, 'I noticed you have branded coasters in all your training rooms'. I explained to her these were most likely made by a promotional merchandise company and we have trained over ten of the biggest in the industry. She gave me her supplier's name and number without hesitation. They were already a client of mine, but it's better that I had asked.

If you want to be referred, make it as easy as possible for your client to refer you. One way to ask is as follows: 'Who would you recommend in terms of your clients/ your suppliers/previous places you used to work that could benefit from what I do?' At least this will focus your client's mind on three areas to which they may be able to refer you.

The clearer and more specific you can be, the better. If you can break down to your clients an average referral, a good referral and a champagne referral for you, then that will help.

As our clients are busy and this is not a key priority for them, it's good to be able to offer them a gift in return for their kind efforts. Some clients will appreciate a financial offer, like some commission on the back of any business that is generated from their introduction; some may prefer a gift or money off their next purchase of your products or services.

A word of warning: some companies have gift regulations, where they are not allowed to accept gifts, as it's seen as bribery. If you are unsure, then just ask your client.

One of my clients created a fake cheque, with their client's name written on it for £250, and it was enclosed in a handwritten card that explained they will get a real cheque for £250 by simply referring any business that could benefit from the IT software they sold. They clearly outlined the ideal types of companies for them, with the right decision-maker contact they aim at. They sent these cards out every other month for six months to their client base of over a thousand businesses and generated over 40 brand new opportunities as a result of their efforts. With an average order value of £85,000 and a 70% conversion rate from a meeting to a sale, you can work out the revenue that was generated from this simple, yet effective, marketing idea.

The key point is asking the question. One tip I was given many years ago was, set a weekly reminder alarm that every week, on that day at 08:30 a.m., you will call one client and ask them for a referral, using one of the techniques that I have just mentioned in this chapter.

24
FAB Selling

'Problems are not stop signs, they are guidelines'.
—Robert H. Schuller

One of the most common mistakes salespeople tend to make is known as 'feature bashing', where they tell the prospective customer all the features of their products and services, and hope that will persuade the prospect to buy. In fact, it achieves the exact opposite.

Imagine a mobile phone salesman doing a pitch to a lady that has walked into their store looking for a new phone. The salesman shows the prospect a new iPhone and says, 'This is our top selling and most popular handset. It has the best camera, amazing memory capacity for you to save loads of pictures and videos and a really wide screen to clearly view all your emails. It has over 300 ringtone options, and comes in grey, black, white and pink'.

The prospect replies, 'I need the handset for my mother, who is 84 years old, and it should be the simplest phone to keep for her security and emergencies'.

What should the salesperson have said when the prospect said they are looking for a new phone? One good question should have been, 'Whom are you looking to buy the phone for?', rather than just making an assumption.

Once the salesman knew it was for an 84-year-old lady, he could have said, 'What features would she like on the phone?' That would have allowed the prospect to open up and tell the salesman everything he needed to know to make that sale.

I made a very similar mistake about 15 years ago when I first set up my training company. An estate agent called me and said, 'They have about 14 branches and over 50 negotiators who require sales training'. The head of HR from the agency said she had been asked by the MD to get three quotes from training companies, and asked why she should select the Tony Morris International to deliver the training.

I thought, *I've got her here.* I said, 'We specialise in sales training, and property is one of the main markets in which we work. All our trainers are under 35 years of age, and they are able to relate to your negotiators well. Finally, all our training is 100% bespoke and therefore can be tailored around your agency'.

She said, 'You are clearly not the right training company for us.'

Shocked and confused, I replied in a defensive tone, 'What do you mean? Why not?' She said, 'The other training companies have worked in an array of industries and this is really important to me and the MD, as they will have a wealth of experience and innovative ideas to bring to the table. You mentioned you specialise in sales training and once our negotiators are trained, we wanted to look at a management training course and customer service course for our property management division'.

In my head I was thinking this – firstly, we have trained in over 40 industries in our first year of trading, and therefore could bring hundreds of new and dynamic ideas to their agency. Secondly, we deliver 12 courses to include management and customer services. However, by opening my mouth and puking all over the prospective customer, with things I thought they'd want to hear, I lost the opportunity. I would look a little desperate and contradict my earlier claims if I was to say we do that and we work in loads of industries.

Now, although this could have been one of the biggest clients I'd ever won and I could have gone into a state of depression, ready to quit sales, I chose to learn from it instead. This situation has arisen again four times, and I'm pleased to say I've won three of them, so overall I have gained more business on the back of losing that opportunity than winning it. Would you label that as failure?

Every time I hear that question asked (why should we select Tony Morris International to deliver the training?), my immediate response is, 'There are many reasons our clients choose us. What are you looking for from a training provider?'

Once I hear their answers, I can explain the benefits we can bring to the table and ensure I include all of their key priorities within my answers, citing examples.

James Dyson, the famous British industrial designer who invented the world's first bagless vacuums, is one of the finest examples of features, advantages and benefits (FAB) selling I have ever seen. In the late 1980s and early 1990s, when Dyson failed countless times to sell his invention to all the major manufacturing companies, he had to mortgage his property three times to continue funding his R&D and to get financial backing by the major companies. Dyson's big break came on *Tomorrow's World*, where his product was demonstrated alongside the standard vacuum cleaner.

Dyson knew the target audience for his product were women, in particular, housewives. Many housewives had children, so what's the most important thing to housewives with children? – the health and safety of their children.

So, on *Tomorrow's World*, the presenter placed two large strips of carpet on one side of the studio and covered it with carpet dust. She began to vacuum one half of the carpet with a standard vacuum cleaner, and then used a Dyson on the other half. She proved that the Dyson picked up 20% more carpet dust than the ordinary vacuum cleaner.

She then turned to the audience and said, 'Ladies and gentleman, are you aware that 80% of children's asthma- and bronchitis-related illnesses are caused by too much carpet dust in the home?'

This alone, combined with the fact that Dyson did not require the continuing purchase of replacement bags, was one of the major reasons behind Dyson becoming the fastest selling vacuum cleaner ever made in the UK.

If we analyse this real-life example, where does FAB selling fit in?

Feature – Cyclone technology.
Advantage – Picks up 20% more carpet dust than any other vacuum cleaner.
Benefit – It reduces your children's risk of getting affected by an asthma- and bronchitis-related illness.

We buy the product of the product; we don't buy what the product is, we buy what the product does. For example, in case of insurance, we buy the protection and security for our family.

- Features – What products have.
- Advantages – What features do.
- Benefits – What features mean.

This was best described to me as follows: you don't go to a hardware store to buy a 12-inch drill; you go to a hardware store to buy a 12-inch hole. The customer wants the result of the product/service they are buying. They want to put their plasma TV on the wall, for that they need a hole, so they go to a hardware store.

Therefore, your job as a professional salesperson is to find out what's important to your prospect and why, and then highlighting the key features, advantages and benefits that your product/service has to offer.

Remember, when you talk about the price, you are discussing the features; when you are talking about the value, you are discussing the benefits it brings to that individual.

The best way to turn a feature into an advantage and then a benefit is to remember these two words: 'which means'. Imagine you are selling crockery to an office manager. In the meeting, you find out the one thing that is very important to him is his budget and, where possible, he needs to keep his costs down. You point out that one feature of your mugs is that they are made with very thick China and are therefore very robust. The advantage of this is that they will last longer than most ordinary mugs, *which means* they won't need replacing as often and will save you money in the long term.

I would recommend listing all the unique features of your products/services and then work out the advantages and benefits for your prospective customers, in order to have these FAB statements ready when needed.

Once you have outlined these, they can help you communicate your unique selling points (USPs). Though, I have an issue with the USP. Any idea why?

Let me ask you this; who does the USP service?

I'll give you a clue, not the prospect. It might be unique, but it's a selling point, as in, you use it to sell. And no one likes to be sold to. I believe it is unique customer benefit (UCB). It is still unique, but it serves our customers, not ourselves.

Many people struggle to articulate their UCBs; if you're one of those people, ask your customers. After all, they're the ones who bought from you or your company and, surely, they're the ones whose opinions matter the most.

Next time you win a customer, turn around and say, 'Thank you for choosing to do business with me. We are always interested on our clients' perspective. For the sake of our learning, please tell why did you decide to work with us, over anyone else?'

Now zip up and start learning.

25
Cross-Selling and Upselling

'An idea without a plan is a dream'.

—Larry Elder

Many people are not clear on the actual difference between 'cross-selling' and 'upselling', and often think they are the same thing. One of the best examples of the difference would have been carried out on you at least once.

At McDonald's, you can be both upsold and cross-sold in the same order.

'For only 30p, would you like to go large on your drink?' This is a perfect example of being upsold to. Very simply, the salesperson persuades you to spend more on the items you were looking to buy.

'Would you like fries with that?' This is a fine example of being cross-sold a product that complements what you are buying.

I remember as a teenager going into Halfords to buy my first mountain bike. I had roughly £90 to spend that I saved up for about two years. I excitedly looked at all the bikes and wanted the coolest looking one with all the bright colours.

The salesman approached me and asked what I was looking for. I said, 'I want a bike to go riding with my friends and it needs to look really cool'.

Ignoring my childish request, he asked where I would ride the bike. Unsure of the relevance, I said, 'There's a forest behind where we live that has great jumps and dirt tracks to ride'. He asked if there was anywhere else I might end up taking the bike. I said, 'My friends and I plan on going camping for weekends away and cycle in the new forest, as it's great and hilly'. He said, 'Now I truly understand what you are looking for and the type of cycling you'll be doing, I would strongly recommend looking at these bikes in particular'. He took me over to a different range that all came in really dull colours. He explained that they had wider tyres, which were much better for off-road cycling, and that the saddle was really well cushioned, which was ideal for maximum comfort when doing jumps.

He explained that it was £35 more than what I was looking at, but it could handle the sort of activities I was planning, whereas the other bikes were better suited for riding on the road. Once he showed me how I could use all 21 gears to improve my performance, I was sold.

Create the Need and Fill It

He qualified me well to understand my real needs, and then was able to 'upsell' by recommending the right bike for me. He made it very easy for me to justify the extra £35 in my head.

As he was walking to the till with me, he asked what protective gear I had, as I was doing a lot of off-road riding and dangerous jumps. He showed me the new graphite helmet, which he explained all the professional riders wear when doing jumps, and then he showed me all the cool colours that I could choose from. He said, 'I assume you'll be taking the bike in the house with you for security?'

I said, 'Only if I want to live in the garden, as my mum would kick me out'. So out came the D-Lock. When I baulked, he asked, 'What's cheaper, laying out another £125 for a bike, or £14.99 to give you peace of mind?'

After buying a water bottle, gloves with air pockets, a D-Lock, a graphite helmet, a sweat-absorbent t-shirt and the off-road mountain bike, I almost puked when I saw the total price of £179.99, especially when I only had £95 on me.

When my dad came to drop off the extra £85, he said, 'He saw you coming a mile off', and it wasn't until I got into sales that I understood what he meant.

I just remember thinking how helpful and knowledgeable the sales guy was, and that I would have recommended him to all my friends.

I had to work in McDonald's for about two months with many extra orders of fries and large meals to pay my dad back, mind you.

One of the first creators of 'cross-selling' online was Amazon. If you have shopped online with Amazon, which I am going to make a wild assumption you have, and which is why Jeff Bezos is worth around $122 billion, you would have noticed the very intelligent software that tells you what products people have bought or looked at, when purchasing the products you have chosen. This is a very discreet and effective way of 'cross-selling', where most consumers feel like Amazon is helping them out, as opposed to being sold too. If, like me, you are the sort of person who always buys something Amazon recommends based on your purchase, then you have also fallen for this innovate 'cross-selling' technique.

During the pandemic, I had to stop golf lessons, as it was during the lockdown times. I had to persuade my wife to get a golf net in the garden. One of the toughest negotiations in my life, and I got the net, but she got a daily massage for three weeks, a bath-run every day for a month, with a glass of wine on demand and both weekend lie-ins for three weeks. I am not sure who negotiated better.

When I browsed Amazon to purchase the golf net for £49.99, I added it to the basket and it said, 'Customers who have bought this have also bought this plastic grass, so you don't rip up your garden'. I thought for only £14.99, it will save one argument with my wife. As the plastic grass went into the basket, it recommended the three rubber tees of different sizes that can be used on the fake grass, so you can practise all your clubs. And then came the multi-coloured rubber balls, in case I was to miss the net, a rubber golf ball couldn't do as much damage to the conservatory.

Suffice to say, £125 later, I was done. The Tiger Woods Nike t-shirt was probably unnecessary, but it really did look good on him. Now of course I was sold to; however, I appreciate the suggestions, the net without the gear would not have been sufficient.

How can we use this technique in our selling, which I have aptly named the 'Amazon technique'? When you sell clients a product or service, say to them, 'Clients who have bought this have also benefited from A, B and C. Shall I add those to your order?'

I train a pharmaceutical company that is best known for selling support products in pharmacies (e.g., elbow supports, knee supports, etc.) They have over 1500 products to offer to their clients, and before training their average order value was £230 per pharmacy.

I had them to review their product range and work out which products complemented each other. There was a muscle-strain gel that was very beneficial if you pulled a muscle and were required to wear a support. Now the salesperson while selling the supports would say, 'Clients of mine who bought the elbow supports really benefited from the muscle-strain gel as well. How many sachets would you like to add to your order?' This increased their average order value to over £300.

In almost 70% of cases, they were able to recommend certain products, which complemented the ones which the customer was looking at. This worked equally well if a product was out of stock, as they were able to say, 'This is out if stock; however, many clients who bought this have found these products just as beneficial'.

26
Handling Rejection

'It may not be your fault for being down, but it's got to be your fault for not getting up'.

—Steve Davis

One inevitable part of sales that can never be avoided is rejection. However, it's only rejection if you label it rejection. Many people say, 'The person is not rejecting you; they are rejecting the idea, product or service that you are proposing'. I completely disagree with this concept, and agree that they are 100% rejecting you.

So, you need to review the call and think. Did I sound boring? Did I sound disinterested? Did I have a good enough opening gambit that engaged the prospect and created some desire?

If the person wasn't rejecting you, then why do some people take a sales call, and some don't? Is it purely on the product or service that's being offered? Of course not.

It's imperative that you do not take it personally, otherwise sales is not right for you. If you get upset every time someone puts the phone down on you or is rude to you, then you are definitely in the wrong profession. You require rhino skin, yet equally you don't keep calling and getting rejected until one person is receptive to you. You review, tweak, dust yourself off and try again. Remember, 'perfect practice makes perfect'.

Not what most people believe, 'practice makes perfect'. If you saw me hit 100 golf balls badly in the range, and then saw me mess up on a golf course, you'll understand that if I kept on practising my awful swing, I would not get anywhere fast, but if I was shown by a professional how to swing properly, then it's worth practising that.

It's only rejection if you label it rejection. So, if my objective of the call is to make an appointment, and I walk away with the decision-maker's name and number, then that's a result. Alternatively, I may make 50 calls, in all of which I may decide they have no requirement for what I'm selling. Rather than walk away feeling rejected, I view it as I had to make those 50 calls at some point, and at least I have got them out the way and can move on.

'Failure's not the falling down, but the staying down'.

As I mentioned earlier, there is no such thing as rejection, it is feedback. Change 'I failed' to 'I've learned what never to do again'. Many salespeople view 'no' as one step closer to a 'yes'.

When you get rejected, go back to the prospect and say, 'I appreciate we are not doing business at this juncture; however, so that I can learn from this and my company can improve and develop, what could I have done differently to be successful?'

The day is not bad unless you name it bad. Rather than investing your time and energy moaning about something, use your creativity to think of a solution.

27
Six Components of Success

'If you dream it, you can do it'.

—Walt Disney

No matter what job you do, whether you are in sales, administration, customer services, sports, films, etc., I believe there are six key components to be successful. I will go on to substantiate this with examples of some of the world-famous people.

I want you to think about whomever you admire, and possibly aspire to be. Anyone you look up to and respect beyond any doubt. Please make a note of these people you have in your mind now.

As you look at that list of people you admire, I want you to identify six key things you feel they all have in common and give them that winning edge over others in their field. Please make a note of these six qualities in the table provided in Figure 27.1:

1.
2.
3.
4.
5.
6.

Figure 27.1

Now compare these qualities mentioned in the following list and see how many of these you got right:

- Positive attitude
- Knowledge
- Pride in themselves or their company
- Enthusiasm
- Self-discipline
- Desire to succeed

I left something out on purpose. It is not something I believe you need to be successful, it helps; however, it is proven you can be successful without it. Any ideas?

Talent

In his book *Bounce: The Myth of Talent and the Power of Practice*, Matthew Syed talks about the idea that talent is not what separates the top performers from the rest, they are the six components outlined in the preceding text.

I don't want to offend any big fans of Geri Halliwell who are reading this book; however, I do not agree she is the most talented singer in this world. She has sold over 12 million records worldwide, yet she can barely hold a tune.

She knew exactly what niche in the music industry she was targeting, and she had so much enthusiasm and a positive attitude, it bordered on annoyance. She created 'girl power' and had so much belief in what the girls represented. She has been extremely disciplined throughout her life and is worth an estimated £18 million from her successful career.

This is a girl from Watford who still cannot hold a tune. Take someone like Madonna, whether you love her or hate her, she is naturally talented, yet has every single one of those six components and is worth an estimated £650 million. The point I am making is, although it helps to be naturally gifted and born with a talent, it's not a key component of success.

Take Katie Price aka Jordan as a fine example. Would you say she is talented? We could all have a pair of implants for £3000 if we chose to, yet she was the first of the many celebrity models to set the trend. Don't get me wrong, my wife makes me watch *What Katie Did Next*, and Jordan is an absolute PR genius. She is clearly intelligent, extremely hardworking and knows how to work a crowd. She has been a huge success and continues to be so with very little to no talent.

Take someone like the late Amy Winehouse, an absolute raw talent and one of the best singers of our generation, but no discipline whatsoever, and unfortunately the inevitable happened.

In my childhood, Paul 'Gazza' Gascoigne was one of my heroes, an amazing footballer and such a great character, but I'd hardly want my little boy to grow up to emulate him. He's in and out of mental institutions and rarely sober; again, lacking discipline and probably a few more of the key components.

Roger Federer, arguably the best tennis player that has ever lived, has every one of the six components, in addition to being talented.

Tiger Woods was of similar ilk before he started his infidelities and went completely downhill. Self-discipline was the missing component.

The key point here is this; do not stress over not having the natural talent, as long as you focus on the six key components, you will be on your way. I cannot guarantee that if you adhere to all six you will be successful. Although I can guarantee that if you don't adhere to them, you won't be successful.

28
Negotiations

'A wise man is only a fool for a short while'.

—Sun Tzu

The purpose of negotiation is to reach a fair and reasonable compromise, not to try to do the impossible. The ideal aim of negotiations for those involved in the negotiation process is to find new ways of arriving at better outcomes, by working in cooperation with the other side. Negotiating should develop a 'partnership' approach, not an 'adversarial' one.

When my father-in-law, Boyd, and I first set up our business in 2006, we won a small contract with a promotional merchandise company within our first six months. We delivered about four days' sales training at our standard rate (£1200 + VAT per day), and the feedback was exceptional.

They saw an immediate uplift in sales, a real boost in motivation and had a clear return on investment (ROI) within six weeks of the training. Boyd and I went back in to see the client and discuss putting a training programme in place. The feedback he gave was incredible, and in the client's eyes we couldn't have done anything more.

The client agreed the training needed to be continually reinforced and wanted us onsite at least seven days a month. Before Boyd and I started high-fiving each other and doing our success dance, we took out our diaries to start booking dates. He said, 'Obviously, I am expecting a discount for booking seven days a month with you, so what can you offer me?'

This would be our first really big deal for our business and in the first few months that was a very exciting prospect. We initially agreed on our standard rates of £1200 + VAT per day, so Boyd said he'd be happy to offer a 10% discount as a gesture of goodwill, to which the client laughed and explained he was looking to pay £400 a day. Resisting the urge to swear, I bit my tongue and sat in silence as my red face did all the talking. After a few seconds of silence, Boyd said, 'Are you actually serious?', to which the audacious gentleman said, 'Absolutely'.

Both Boyd and I said in unison that it was an impossibility and asked to meet somewhere in the middle, to which the client quickly calculated a day rate of £740 (£1200 − £120 (we agreed) = £1080 − £400 = £680), therefore £400 + £340 = £740. Was this client a genius mathematician, or had this negotiation already been planned out before Boyd and I had even sat down for the meeting?

My guess is the latter.

Whichever way you look at it, this client has cleverly got us to drop our prices by £460 per day without giving anything away. Who was negotiating better at this point?

Our success dance seemed a lot more fun than where we were right now. Boyd jumped in and said, 'If we were to meet you in the middle, how many days would you commit to?' The client replied, 'Let's just do the first seven days, and if the results improve after that, then we can discuss it again'.

I rightly pointed out it was all his way at the moment, and we aren't getting anything in return. He agreed and said he was being unfair, and was happy to commit to four months at seven days a month, but at £450 a day.

And here we were again, back at his price. He knew we were very early on in our new business and our diaries were pretty clear, as Boyd and I had laid out our freshly printed outlook calendars with two dates pencilled out in the entire month. He took advantage of the situation and knew he was in a clear position of strength so could use the famous negotiation card known as 'taking the absolute piss'.

Boyd asked if we could take two minutes to discuss this proposal, and the client agreed. Again, this request demonstrates we were willing even to consider this ludicrous offer, again putting us in the weaker position.

Boyd said he was keen to move forward, as he felt 28 days at £450 is better than a punch in the face and it was £12,600 of business that we could really do with. It was better than what we currently had on the table of nothing.

I strongly disagreed and felt we were devaluing our-selves at agreeing to this rate and said, 'Our time will be better spent focusing on getting business at our normal rate, which we have proven is achievable'.

So after a little row between partners, we agreed to reject the offer and thank the client for his time, with the naive optimism he would beg us to stay and agree to our terms, which, surprisingly, he didn't.

Did we regret our decision? I suppose a bit, but it was a good lesson so early on and it taught us one of the best lessons in negotiations, which is you sometimes must walk away. In an ideal world, both parties will get what they want, but I'm still waiting for loads to happen in my ideal world, to include Angelina Jolie and Liz Hurley.

From this example and many other situations in which my clients and I have found ourselves, there are some key rules to remember in every negotiation.

Rule 1

Always have an alternative, giving you freedom of choice. Whether you are buying or selling, if you can't walk away because you need the deal badly or because the other side is the only game in town, then you are at a serious disadvantage, as Boyd and I proved with our client.

If the other side believes you are the only game in town, then you have the advantage. No other factor is so important; the more you need to secure the deal, the weaker your position, so avoid negotiating when you need the business badly (for the same reason, never find a new house and fall in love with it before you sell your own).

The same will apply to your customer, which is why buyers almost always give you the impression that they can go somewhere else – even if they can't or don't want to.

This also means that when selling, you must create an impression that there is no alternative, comparable supplier. You have to create the impression that your product or service is unique, and that the other person has nowhere else to go. The way you sell yourself and your product must convince the other person that he has nowhere else to go, and that he cannot afford to walk away. So it's vital you know all your unique selling points (USPs) or UCBs as discussed earlier in this book. These should be assessed before the meeting, so you are well-equipped and best prepared.

Some clients have asked me what if their product or service is not unique. These are then called key customer benefits (KCBs) and should still be mentioned and tailored around the client's requirements. If your product offer is not unique, remember that *you* are part of it. You can still create a unique position for yourself by the way you conduct yourself, build trust, rapport and empathy with the other person. I always remind myself they can't find another Tony Morris at any other training company.

Rule 2

Negotiate when the sale is conditionally agreed, and no sooner (buyers tend to try to negotiate before giving you any commitment, don't let them). I wish I had used this advice before going into meeting with our promotional merchandise client. We could have started the meeting by asking a trial close: 'If we can agree on the details today, will you go ahead?'

Rule 3

Aim for the best outcome (buyers aim low, and they tend not to go first). Many negotiations are little more than a split-the-difference exercise. They shouldn't be, but that's often the underlying psychology and expectation. So it's logical that to achieve the best possible finishing position, you should start as ambitiously as you can (without losing credibility, of course). This was the reason for our client's £400 start, which was a 66% drop on our standard rate, where we started with just a 10% drop. We were putty in his hands.

If you have the option to hear the other person's offer first, then do so. It's a fact that whoever makes the opening offer is at a disadvantage. If you go first, the other person can choose to disregard it and ask for a better offer. And the other person avoids the risk of making an offer themselves that is more beneficial than you would have been prepared to accept. It's amazing how often a buyer is prepared to pay more than an asking price, but avoids having to do so because they keep quiet and let the seller go first. The seller can often achieve a higher selling price than he anticipates if he hears what the buyer is prepared to offer first.

Rule 4

Get the other person's full 'shopping list' before you start to negotiate (buyers usually do the opposite; they like to pick concessions up one by one, indefinitely).

Establish in your own mind your client's needs before the meeting. Everything that is part of or related to a deal has a value. Everything has a cost to you or your business, even if it's not on the price list. Negotiation isn't about price and discount. It's about everything that forms the deal, such as:

- Specification
- Colour
- Size
- Lead time
- Contract length
- Penalty payments
- Delivery dates
- Stockholding
- After-sales support
- Product training
- Technical backup

- Call-out costs
- Breakdown costs
- Parts costs
- Payment type and terms
- Payment date

These are called 'variables', and each one affects the cost. Some affect the cost more than others, and buyers and sellers nearly always place a different value on each. It's critical therefore to know exactly what your buyer wants, before you start to negotiate. Get the full list of issues written down and commit him to it. This is vital if you are to keep a track on the values of the deal and the eventual outcome. You also avoid your position being eroded bit by bit by the late introduction of concessions.

Rule 5

Never give away a concession without getting something in return (buyers tend to resist giving any concessions at all). This is one of the most important parts of any negotiation, and it's just a matter of discipline and control. Never give anything away without getting something in return. If you do, you are not negotiating, you are simply conceding. My son Harry, who is currently 14 years old, does it now.

'Harry, go to bed', I say.

'If you let me have some chocolate, I'll go to bed', Harry says.

'Fine, have some chocolate', I say, if the missus isn't in the room.

Then he uses the assumptive alternative close on me, 'Can I have two or three chocolates?'

I am so proud of that little closer.

A commitment from the other person can be a suitable concession to get in return for something of relatively low value. The simplest and most elegant concession to secure is agreement to proceed with the deal now; use it to close.

Rule 6

Keep the whole package in mind at all times. The buyer's tactic will be to separate out single issues, or introduce new ones later. If you allow this to happen, your position will be eroded. Think about the knock-on effects to the whole situation, every time a concession is requested. The overall value and profitability of a deal or contract depend on its component parts. When you change one element, you change the whole, so keep the whole situation in mind. Keep assessing effects on the total arrangement, understand the effects and explain how each change or demand affects the whole thing.

Rule 7

Keep searching for variables, concessions, 'bargaining chips' and incentives (buyers will look for your concessions, but will tend not to offer their own). A variable is any factor that can be altered, and which has a real or perceived value. You are not a mind reader, and the other person may not be totally open or even fully aware of all the possible variables that are of interest, so keep looking for them.

Before the meeting, prepare and estimate values of real and perceived variables, and keep looking for new ones during the negotiation. The more variables you find, the less you will have to give on price, and the more added value you can build into the deal.

Rule 8

Keep accurate notes and show that you are doing it. You want to avoid the 'he said, she said' scenario at all costs. The other person may forget, misunderstand or attempt to distort interpretation of what was discussed and agreed on. Keeping notes shows that you are in control, professional, can't be outflanked, and it enables you to summarise and assess continually.

Rule 9

Summarise and confirm understanding continually, so you are both on the same page. This avoids misunderstandings developing, accidentally or otherwise. Misunderstandings can be catastrophic, not so much because of the way they affect the financial structure of the unfolding deal, but because they undermine the rapport and the trust, which are critical to being able to do business in the first place.

Getting positive agreement throughout the process is also psychologically important; it strengthens trust and commitment and helps to ease the other person into an agreeable frame of mind. After the negotiation, it is essential to email the client clear, written confirmation of the deal and get his/her agreement back.

Sell the Difference

One thing many clients look to do is to compare your offer to your competition when trying to negotiate the deal. It's crucial you find out with whom you are being compared to and what they are offering.

For example, if your product costs £1000 and they feel it's too expensive, find out what you are being compared against. If the competitor's product costs £750, find out exactly what the buyer is getting for that. Then simply sell the additional benefits of your product/service for 'only £250'.

It's really important to stand your ground when negotiating. One great technique is called the 'take away'. If I charge £1500 per day for my training, which includes many things such as the training notes, mystery calls, certificates, etc., and the client asks me to move on my costs, I reply by saying, 'With pleasure. What would you like me to take out of my offer?'

They are not normally expecting this and it really catches them off guard and they question what you mean. I say, 'Well, I can take £150 off, but I won't be able to provide course notes or certificates'.

All these variables have a cost and a perceived value, and you must be ready to trade them with confidence.

Very early on in my sales career, I was on a training course and the participants were split into pairs. We were both given an orange and an envelope each and told to negotiate. In the envelope, it explained that I needed the inside of the orange to make some fresh orange juice, but I was not allowed to disclose this information if questioned. It transpired my partner needed the orange peel to use for a cake, and, again, he was sworn to secrecy. Without knowing how to handle the situation, we ended up cutting the orange in half and thinking that was the ideal 'win-win' for us both. Looking back, if we had just asked each other which part of the orange the other *didn't* need, it would have told us everything and we would have reached the perfect 'win-win'.

29
Time Management

'The most effective way to do it, is to do it'.

—Amelia Earhart

You have probably heard the cliche expression 'work smarter, not harder'. That's great, but no one ever tells you how that's possible. It makes sense that if you are paid to work between 09:00 and 17:30, then you shouldn't need to take work home with you every night or be working on your weekends. Don't get me wrong, I am a big believer in 'what you put in is what you get out', so if you do the bare minimum of what's expected of you, then don't expect to be promoted to the position of the sales director anytime soon. But there needs to be a balance between work life and personal life, and from working with over 36,000 sales professionals, I have compiled a list of things to do to manage your time effectively.

There are only three activities that lead to sales:

1. Prospecting.
2. Telephone and face-to-face appointments.
3. Follow-ups.

Therefore, every task you do, you need to ask yourself, 'Is this crucial now, or should I be doing one of the three?'

There is no such thing as time management. Time is a constant, so it cannot be managed. I believe it is task management. Manage the tasks within the time available.

Every night we must compile a 'will-do' list for the following day. Once we arrive in the office, we need to look at our emails and add things to the 'will-do' list. The most important aspect is to prioritise the 'will-do' list first thing in the morning. Please remember, you prioritise tasks in terms of what is more important, not what is more enjoyable.

As sales professionals, your role is to make calls and sales; without this our business cannot continue. Therefore, we have to spend as much time as possible on the phone, converting enquiries into business or creating opportunities. We need to try where possible and do all quotes and proposals during 'non-phone time' such as 08:30–09:30 and after 17:30. I accept this isn't always achievable; however, this is our challenge and our aim.

The key is we need to be working, when we are working. It's very easy to enter into work chats about our social lives or look on social websites such as Facebook, but is this making the best of our work time?

Most underachievers spend approximately one hour per day having chit-chat and looking up irrelevant websites. This equates to five hours per week, twenty hours per month. How many more calls could you take in twenty hours and turn into business?

One great time saver when making calls is to not put the phone down. I know it sounds obvious, but how many of us actually do that? Next time you make calls, have all the leads ready and once you have made the call, hang up the receiver without putting the phone down and make your next call. I guarantee you can make at least 15% more calls this way, and that could be the difference between success and failure. I observed this strategy in one of my favourite films of all time, *The Pursuit of Happyness* with Will Smith and Jaden Smith. Will plays Chris Gardner, and it's a true story. In the film, Will barely takes a drink, therefore not needing time to go to the toilet. And he never puts the phone down. This enabled him to make more calls than anybody else on the floor.

Lack of motivation and procrastination are the two main causes of underperformance. Next time you go to work, try and be the first one in and the last to leave. Take five minutes less for lunch and see how much more can be achieved.

Finally, ensure all information on the phone goes straight on to your system. There is no value in duplicating work from paper to computer, it simply wastes time.

One estate agent I work with was writing all the information he took on a call down on a pad. When he was quiet, he was using that time to type up all the information onto their bespoke CRM system. On average, he took 45 calls per day and it took approximately three minutes to type up each call. That's 135 minutes a day, 675 minutes a week. If you were given an extra 11 hours a week to work on doing more business, how much extra could you achieve? This client has bought everyone headsets and insisted all notes go straight on to their system. This simple observation and change has increased their revenue by 17% in the past six months.

Here are some key factors for time management:

Turn off the email notification sound and only check emails three times a day (morning, lunch and evening). This is one of the biggest distractions, because not only do you look at your emails, you feel obliged to respond. If anything is ever that urgent, the person would find a way to get in touch with you. I accept for certain jobs you're in, this is not feasible; however, this will be a small percentage of jobs.

Keep a time log for two weeks to identify where you are spending your time and see where it can be improved. The best way to do this is write down on a pad everything you do and record a time next to it. For example:

08:46–08:53	Make breakfast.
08:54–09:19	Check emails and respond.
09:19–09:31	Check diary and write a 'to-do' list.
09:32–09:47	Write a list of calls to make.
09:48	Make first sales call.

Does this look familiar? By working differently, you should be able to make your first sales call at 09:15 and start finding opportunities. Many people feel you shouldn't make sales calls before 10:00, as people have just gone in and will be busy.

People are always busy, so you should always be making sales calls. If you listened to all the times people think are bad times to call – Monday morning, Friday afternoon, Wednesday between 11:00 and 13:00 – you would never pick up the phone. Ask the top sales performers, 'When is the best time to make calls?' You won't be able to, as I guarantee they are on the phone.

Think about every task you do and ask yourself, 'Is there a better way of doing this?'

You may not always be able to find a better way; however, my estate agency client asked himself this question and has created a further 11 hours a week to do more business.

Produce a weekly schedule, so you set other people's expectations and your own. Make sure your line managers see this and are happy with your plans. Once they have seen it and agreed to it, you must not be scared of sticking to it if they come and delegate work to you.

A lot of my clients like the ideas I am suggesting, but they say when their boss comes to their desk and says, 'Do this now', they say it all goes out the window. My answer to this is speak out and say, 'The next two hours I have prioritised to do A, B and C, and unless the task you are asking of me is life or death, I can't do it until 15:00'.

When prioritising your 'will-do' list the night before, ask yourself, 'Is this important or urgent?' Usually, you'll find it's not urgent. But the urgent tasks *must* be completed by the time you set, because surely if they are not, there will be consequences.

If two tasks are of equal importance, then discuss the actual requirements with the people dependent on the tasks' outcomes, and reassess the 'real' urgency and priority of these tasks.

Review your work environment; ensure you have folders set up and file everything away as soon as you have finished with it. Many people say to themselves, 'I'll file it away another time, it can wait'. If you are one of these people, then you need to become disciplined in your approach, as that pile will grow, and things will go missing.

Learn to say 'no' politely and constructively; delegate, if possible, and agree on a realistic deadline.

Probe deadlines to establish the true situation. I lost a big opportunity about a year ago by not ascertaining the deadline. I finished the call on a Tuesday at around

16:50, where the prospect said he was going to use me and his current training provider, to deliver a one day presentation course each and whoever gets the best feedback will win the contract to deliver to his team of 60 salespeople.

He asked me to email him an agenda of exactly what I'll cover and a few dates that I was available to deliver this course. I emailed this over on Wednesday evening after work and called on Friday to book a date in. He said, 'I have given both the days to my current training provider, as you were too slow getting the agenda and dates over to me'. I tried to explain I did it that evening, as he didn't specify when he needed them by, to which he responded, 'You didn't ask'.

Although this guy was clearly an asshole, it's a good lesson learned. I now ask every time, 'Is there a specific time by which you need this back?'

Set up email templates for every eventuality. I touched on this in an earlier chapter and shared some examples. I have about 40 email templates, some I shared with you earlier on in this book. I have created a template for the following situations:

* Meeting confirmation (just change the name, date and time).
* Feedback on proposal.
* Reasons I lost the deal.
* Chasing a proposal when being ignored (I have given this a professional name of 'shit or get off the pot' – the client doesn't see the name).

- Every industry to which I send information will have a template. For example, estate agent industry will use the right language for that industry (applicant, negotiators, valuations, etc.), and will have a testimonial from another estate agent with whom I have worked.
- Thank you for enquiring on my website.
- Contracts or invoices.

Avoid others who waste your time: We all have clients who love to chat. I either avoid them like the plague or choose the right time to speak to them, out of call time, that is, before 08:45 or after 18:00.

Unnecessary Meetings

I am sure you have experienced meetings, for the sake of meetings. If you genuinely feel you don't need to be there, or you are not gaining anything, or not able to add value, then do not be afraid to put that across to your senior. As long as you explain what work you wish to do instead, they should respect your reasoning.

Elephant Tasks

Split big tasks into small digestible chunks and allocate time to each. How many times are you given a big project to do and try and complete it then and there?

Depending on when the deadline is, it's always best to split it into pieces, and do one piece at a time.

Work hardest and prioritise your most important tasks for when you are at your most alert. I am not the best morning person. I have always found I am great at doing proposals or reports late in an evening when I am most relaxed. Try and work out when your best times are and plan around that.

Do proposals and any administration outside of the call times where possible (09:00–13:00 and 14:00–17:30). I accept this is not always going to be achievable; however, many salespeople choose to do these tasks during the day as they prefer it to cold calling or smart calling.

Set specific goals for the day, for example, the number of appointments you can make. As salespeople, we should be goal-driven and it's important to treat every day as a fresh new opportunity, as we never know what it could bring. I feel it's really important and motivational to set specific goals you want to achieve every day, no matter how big or small.

Create power hours in the day where all you do is cold calling. If a part of your role is to generate new business and one of the ways you achieve that is by smart calling, then I would recommend splitting your day into power hours. It can be quite demoralising spending a solid six hours on the phone without a break. It's much more effective to do five to six power hours throughout the day, where in that hour you give it your 100% undivided attention.

The final point is to plan your week on the week-end before. For example, if I know I have a three-hour train journey on a Tuesday morning and a three-hour return journey on Thursday evening, I will plan to do proposals or administration tasks in those six hours, rather than in the evening or during call time.

If I know on a Wednesday that I have a new prospect meeting two hours from my office, I will plan to prospect around that area to make the most of my time out of the office. If I am unable to make any new business meetings, I will see which clients I have in and around that area to visit and get more work or gain referrals.

If you can take all these points onboard and put them into practice, I guarantee you will find you have more time on your hands than you do at present.

30

Gaining Commitment and Closing

'Setting goals is the first step in turning the invisible into the visible'.

—Tony Robbins

There is no point working hard, doing a wonderful opening, getting the fact-find right, selling the benefits and *not* asking for the order. It would be like a footballer kicking the ball towards the goal and then being disappointed that the goalie didn't just walk out the way and let the ball in the net. No one is going to do it for you.

Customer says, 'I won't proceed now because my budget is too tight'. This is a buying signal that you must deal with. Establish if this is genuine. The customer likes what you are offering, but budget is stopping him. Ensure that this is the only thing stopping him going ahead today, probe to find out how his budget works and then close him.

We all need to know when to close, as well as how to close; timing plays a very big part in your success. If you close before your customer has all the information he needs, you will fail to achieve your goals.

Please don't be frightened to fail; you can't win the lottery without buying a ticket.

About a year ago, I was training a tour operator and the sales team was responsible for taking inbound calls for people looking to book holidays. I was undertaking live telephone coaching and was sitting with a girl called Laura, who I can honestly say was one of the best sales professionals I had ever worked with. She was extremely organised and methodical; she could build rapport with all types of customers she conversed with, from the 19-year-old student to the 74-year-old man. There was one call in particular where she was speaking to a lady about a £60,000 holiday, as she was enquiring on behalf of five families. Laura built a wonderful rapport with her in a matter of minutes and put this woman at ease. She questioned her brilliantly without coming across as a salesperson, just showing she was interested and being consultative. The lady threw a couple of objections at her like, 'I've had a cheaper quote and I need to go away and speak to my friends', and Laura dealt with both with absolute style. It was about a 20-minute call and towards the end Laura said to the lady, 'You have been speaking with Laura Hamilton and if you wish to book, my direct line is ... I hope to hear from you soon. Goodbye'.

Laura put her headset down and looked at me and in a sweet cheeky way said, 'I'm pretty good, aren't I?' I said, 'You are better than pretty good, but why didn't you ask if she'd like to go ahead and book?' Laura replied, 'I am pleased you are here to train and develop us; however, you will not make me a pushy salesperson. I have never been like that, it's not my style and I never want to become like one of those cheesy salespeople'.

Confused, I said, 'What do you mean?'

She said, 'I am open to your advice, yet I don't want to learn ways to become pushy'.

I spoke with her boss and the head of the 34-seat call centre, and it transpired that Laura normally finished 12th every month in terms of sales performance. She was not only by far the best salesperson in that room, she was one of the best with whom I had ever worked. However, in her head it was pushy and cheesy to ask for the business. When questioned much further, she fell into the same trap as over 90% of salespeople for the reason they don't ask for the business – fear of rejection.

When I looked at Laura's traffic light pipeline, she had no deals in hot, about three deals bubbling in warm and about 120 deals in cold, which she called her 'maybe column'. It was only a 'maybe column', as she hadn't asked if they would like to go ahead.

If you don't ask, you don't get.

I am a massive believer in this, and if you don't ask, you don't know what concerns the prospects may have, and, therefore, don't get an opportunity to deal with them. Not asking does not only hinder your performance it stops you getting feedback, which will help develop you as a sales professional.

Closing is not just about asking for the business, it's about getting commitment and achieving your goal, such as making an appointment. In many of my training sessions, I get a delegate I call 'the neg', whose main objective is to cause disruption and show the team the reason he/she doesn't need training, as they know it all. They often say, 'You couldn't close me, as I only buy if I want something specifically, I'm NOT closable'.

My standard response is I pull out a fiver and say, 'If I can close, will you give me a fiver?' They fall for what I thought was an obvious trap and say, 'Yeah, but you won't be able to'. This is how I earn the majority of money from training, so the more 'negs', the better.

So, the main thing to remember about closing is *ask*. If you have done everything else we have talked about right, the majority of the time the deal will close itself.

So for those occasions where the prospect needs that gentle push, here are some great techniques to use.

Examples of Some Closing Techniques

Assumptive close: Assume the order. Don't say, 'Do you want it?' Say, 'When do you want it?'

Imagine you sell pens for a living. Rather than saying to the prospect, 'Would you like to go ahead?', to which they could respond with 'No', you would ask any of these assumptive closes:

'How many pens would you like to order?'
'What colour would you like the pens in?'
'What date would you like delivery of the pens?'
'Whose names shall I put on the invoice?'
'From the different styles of pens we have been discussing, which one do you want to go ahead with?'

Alternative close: 'Which day is best to meet, Tuesday or Thursday?'

This is the best type of close for making an appointment. Again, if you ask 'Would you like to meet me?', it is giving the prospect the option to say 'no'. Whereas if the only option is 'What day should we meet?', you are likely to get a positive response.

Third-party proof close: Tell them how well you worked with another company, letting them know the benefits it will bring them. This will give them more confidence in what you are saying and make it easier to say, 'Can you see how this would work for you, Mr . . .?' Once they have said, 'Yes', you would then say 'That's great! What we need to do now is. . .'. This is where testimonials come into their own. When you talk about how good you are, it's 'bragging', but when someone else talks about how good you are, it's 'proof'. Every proposal you send out should include a testimonial relevant to the industry or a business that had the same challenge as the one to whom you are pitching, and, most importantly, a testimonial about how you specifically helped them overcome this challenge. The more specific the testimonial, the better. For example, 'Our sales increased by 37% and our customer attrition reduced from 14% to 3% in one year'.

Trial close: 'If I can, will you go ahead today?'

This is one of the most commonly used techniques, and is very effective if used correctly. It gives the impression that the customer is getting a great deal and you have gone especially out of your way to help them. I used to train a loan company whose customers were in serious debt. They offer annual percentage rate (APR) rates of 19%, which were extremely high, but the customers were unable to get approval for loans elsewhere. The salespeople were told by management that if a customer asks for a discount, they were allowed to drop the APR rate to 17%, and that's only as the last resort to getting the sale.

Prior to training, whenever a customer asked for a cheaper rate, the salesperson would say, 'We can do it for 17%', and more often than not the customer would say, 'Thanks, I want to go away and get other quotes'.

After training, when they learned the trial close, the conversation would go more like this:

SALESPERSON: We can offer you a loan for £7000 with 19% APR.

CUSTOMER: That rate seems awfully high, how much can you reduce that to?

SALESPERSON: Well, unfortunately there is no movement, 19% is our standard rate. I am happy to go away and speak to my director, but it's very unlikely they'll do anything. *If I can get him to reduce it at all, will you go ahead with the loan today?*

CUSTOMER: Yes, if you can get a discount, I'll take the loan

SALESPERSON: Okay, well, I can't promise anything, but I will try my best for you.

An hour later. . .

SALESPERSON: I am really pleased to say my director was happy for me to reduce it by 2%, as you agreed to take the loan out today. Now all I need to do is fill out some paperwork with you.

Direct close: 'Are you ready to move forward?'
This is probably the best close to use for people who fall into the red behaviour, as they don't like waffle and want someone to be straight to the point. The diverse types of direct closes are:

Can I have your business?
Can we move forward?

Reverse close: If someone asks, 'How much is your training?' I would respond by saying, 'Well, how many days do you want to book?'

This close is used when a question is asked of you, which is a buying signal. I work with a courier company and they often get asked, 'How much do you charge for up to 15 kg?' They now respond, 'How many shipments do you have?'

Probability close: 'On a scale of 1–10, 10 being you are ready to proceed, where are you on that scale? What do I need to do to move you from a 7 to a 10?'

This is a good technique to use in a face-to-face meeting. It helps you ascertain what the prospect is thinking at that particular time and helps them open up. It may invite some objections, but you need to get these out in the open and dealt with before proceeding to a sale.

Preventative close: 'Is there any reason why we shouldn't move forward with this?'

A great close to use to get straight to the point, and again uncover any concerns or objections. You will normally get a positive response, to which you then explain to the prospect what the next steps are to complete the sale.

Open close: What do I need to do to. . .

'Win your business?'
'Work with you?'
'Move this forward?'

Use the ending with which you are most comfortable and the one most appropriate for the behaviour you are dealing with. A red behaviour would appreciate the top answer if it's their company, as it strokes their ego by asking to win their business. A green behaviour would prefer the other two endings.

It's all very well closing, but one of the most vital parts of the sale that many salespeople forget is 'consolidation'. We said in smart calling that the first five seconds of every call are vital. Well, it's an absolute fact that the last five seconds are just as, if not more, important. You want the customer to put the phone down and say, 'I am really happy with. . ., and what a great guy/girl he/she was'. They are now a happy buyer and will remember you. Please remember, if this is done properly, it is at this stage you would ask for referrals and 'upsell', if and where appropriate.

The other thing to remember when it comes to closing is 'it's not about you'. When I ask salespeople, what is the reason you don't close, these are the typical responses:

'I don't want to appear pushy'.
'I don't want to get a no'.
'I don't want to appear desperate'.

If you look at these three responses, who are they talking about?

Themselves.

Think about the perception the prospect has of the salesperson that does NOT ask for the business:

They clearly do not want to work with me.
They obviously do not think they can help.
I am clearly not a big enough customer for them.

So, next time your inner voice starts telling you the reasons to NOT ask for the business, I want you to think about it through your prospect's lens, not your own.

31
Howlers

'You can't build a reputation on what you are going to do'.
—Henry Ford

In my 22-year sales career, I have made some major howlers that are amusing and worth sharing. These are all sadly true and some beyond embarrassing; however, I feel we have now bonded and I'm happy to share.

My First B2B Sales Job

My first business-to-business (B2B) sales role was selling IT software in London, and I was 21 years of age. I started as a telesales rep and my role was to make appointments from cold calling for the field sales reps. I remember in my first week, my boss and the sales director of the company asked me 'to take the sales board down', as it was the end of the month. Although I thought it was a bizarre request, I wasn't about to question my brand new boss. I went and asked one of the systems engineers to borrow a screwdriver, and it took about 15 minutes to take the board down, as I was never great at 'do it yourself' (DIY).

I took the board into my boss's room and, struggling to hold this huge white board, asked, 'Where would you like me to put it?'

He looked at me like I was insane and said, 'What the hell do you think you're doing?'

'As you asked, I took the board down'.

'No, you moron, I meant wipe the month off and put the new dates on for the forthcoming sales month!'

I couldn't see my own face, but I could feel the heat radiating off it in sheer embarrassment. I walked out of his office, put the board back up and never shared this with anyone.

My First Field Meeting

After eight months, I was promoted to a field sales rep and had a telesales rep appointed to make meetings for me. The first meeting my telesales rep made was at a football club, and I was asked to attend with one of the more senior sales reps to make sure I was doing things correctly. I remember when we stepped into the IT director's office, I panicked as the desk was such a tip, I didn't know where to sit and place my things. The gentleman cleared some room on his desk and said, 'Please take a seat and ignore the mess, I have just moved in to this office'.

The meeting went okay and although we didn't get the business, we qualified him really well and organised for him to trial our software, which was one of my objectives. After about an hour, the meeting had come to its natural end, and I put my meeting book away in my leather folder, shook the guys hand and thanked him for his time.

I returned back to the office and went and sat down with my sales director to give him feedback on the meeting. Whilst in my boss's office, one of the telesales reps knocked at the door and said, 'The director of X is on the phone and needs to speak to Tony as a matter of urgency'. My sales director looked at me with that worried look, and I apologised and ran to the phone. The IT director asked if I had taken his meeting book. Shocked and taken aback, I replied, 'Of course not', and checked my leather folder and of course I had. Due to the state of the guy's desk, I mistakenly left my meeting book and had taken his. I apologised profusely and agreed to drive back immediately to exchange them. Cosmic!

Call Centre Selling Gas and Electric

I have worked in many call centres in my time, just to earn some extra pocket money. One of them was the biggest outsourced call centres in the UK and I worked on the utilities campaign, where my job was to switch people over from their current supplier to another provider.

It was all business-to-customer (B2C), and we were phoning people at home. In addition to the commission, they gave us incentives, such as you were allowed to leave early when you hit your target.

One hot summer's day, we were all desperate to leave before our 17:00 finish, I was smashing the phones, desperate to make my final sale. It was 13:15 and I was on my ninth sale and just couldn't get hold of anybody to pitch. I then had one of those light bulb moments and thought of the easiest sale in the world who will definitely be home – my Grandma Betty.

ME:	Hi, Grandma, it's Tony, you okay?
GRANDMA BETTY:	Who, darling?
ME:	It's me, Grandma, Tony, can you hear me?
GRANDMA BETTY:	Oh, hi, Tony, I can hear you now, you okay?
ME:	Yeah, I'm great thanks, Grandma. I need a big favour. You know that company I work for? Well, when you hit all your sales, they let you go home early and I have one sale left to do. So, please can you just agree to move over to X and when the paperwork comes through in seven days, I will come round to your flat and cancel it for you.
GRANDMA BETTY:	Who's X, darling?

ME:	Don't worry, it's not relevant, and I must pass you over to the verifier who will ask you if you are happy to move over to them and just say 'yes', is that okay?
GRANDMA BETTY:	I'm with British Gas though, sweetheart.
ME:	I know you are Grandma, but don't worry you will stay with them. You just have to say to this guy you are happy to swap, and then they will send out paperwork to your flat and I will come round and personally call up and cancel it for you.
GRANDMA BETTY:	Oh, okay then, so what do I need to do?
ME:	I'm just going to pass you over to this man who will ask you your name and just want to confirm you are happy to switch over to and that's it.

I passed the phone over, grabbed my bag and turned off my computer. I had already starting jesting with my mates that they had to stay all day and I was off to play footie in the park.

VERIFIER:	Good afternoon, am I speaking to Betty Morris?
GRANDMA BETTY:	Yes, who's this?

VERIFIER:	My name is Sunny Patel and I just need to confirm you are happy to move your gas and electric over from British Gas to X.
GRANDMA BETTY:	I'm happy with British Gas, thank you.
VERIFIER:	I understand that, but Tony has explained that you are happy to move over to X.
GRANDMA BETTY:	No, I want to stay where I am, thank you.
VERIFIER:	Okay, I'm just going to have to put you on hold for a minute please. Tony, Mrs Morris is saying she is happy with British Gas and doesn't want to move to X.
ME:	What, that's not possible. Let me speak to her a second. Grandma, it's Tony again, what's wrong?
GRANDMA BETTY:	I didn't realise I had to move over and I'm happy with British Gas, darling.
ME:	I know you are, grandma, but as I said, you won't have to swap over. Just agree to it now, and I promise I will come round when you get the paperwork and I will call them up and cancel it for you. Is that okay?

GRANDMA BETTY:	Okay, darling, I understand. Pass the gentleman back then?
VERIFIER:	Hello again, Mrs Morris. So can I now confirm you are happy to switch to X?
GRANDMA BETTY:	Yes, that's fine.
VERIFIER:	Great, I just need to confirm that your address is ___.
GRANDMA BETTY:	Yes, it is.
VERIFIER:	Excellent. All I need now is to take the long number on your credit card, please.
GRANDMA BETTY:	Credit card, I'm not paying for anything now. No, I'm sorry, I want to leave things how they are.
VERIFIER:	I do need to take your details just to put this transaction through. No money is taken; it's just required to set up your direct debit.
GRANDMA BETTY:	No, let's leave it, please. I don't want to give my credit card details out over the phone.
VERIFIER:	Okay, you're just going to have to hold the line again, Mrs Morris. Tony, she doesn't want to give me her credit card details. We're going to have to leave this, I'm afraid.

ME:	Bloody hell, let me have another word with her. Grandma, it's me again. What's wrong this time?
GRANDMA BETTY:	I don't want to give that gentleman my credit card details. God knows what he'll do with them, and I don't trust anybody who asks for my credit card details on the phone. Thieves, the lot of them.
ME:	He's not trying to rob you, grandma. He has to take your details to put the deal through. As I said, I'll cancel it all, nothing will leave your account. If you want, I'll give you my credit card details to give to the man.
GRANDMA BETTY:	No, darling, it's all too complicated. Let's just leave it now. Anyway, what are you doing today, sweetheart?
ME:	Looks like I'm working all day. Speak to you later, Grandma.

Double Glazing

When I was at university, I did a couple of sales jobs just to earn some extra beer money. In my first year, I got an evening job selling double glazing over the phone. On my first evening, I went to the offices, and they explained the pitch and said I had to get commitment from the customer to have a free, no obligation quote and had to organise a date and time for one of the field reps to go over to their property.

Eager to get on the phone, I started banging out the calls, desperate to impress my new boss and my fellow peers, and be the first to make an appointment that evening. Every call I made, they either had double glazing or the phone got put down by the time I said, 'It's Tony, calling from . . .'.

But I knew the first rule of sales is 'not to give up and keep making the calls'. After about an hour, I got hold of this sweet old lady who was more than happy to take my call, and she started telling me what she had made for dinner and was moaning about how bad TV was these days.

I tried to listen without sounding as bored as I was and once I realised she was repeating the same story, I decided to take control of the call and interjected by saying, 'Mrs Maddox, the reason for my call this evening is to offer you a free, no obligation quote, to get double glazing in your property'.

'Is that completely free of charge, dear?' she asked.

'Absolutely, Mrs Maddox, won't cost you a penny. I just need to arrange a date and time convenient for you for my rep to come around, and that's all there is to it'.

'Sounds great, let me just get my diary, won't be a minute dear', she said.

I stood up, doing my closing dance and gave myself high fives. My boss excitedly high-fived me and said to go ring the bell, which was located at the front of the office for all to see.

I got a big cheer when the bell rang and a standing ovation from the eight salespeople in the room, as I was new to the team. Like an overexcited schoolboy, I continued to finish my closing dance in front of my jeering peers, which involved a lot of bum shaking and hip movement. As I went to pull off my final move, the rep shouted out my name.

'Tony, were you aware Mrs Maddox lives in a block of flats?'

'Yes', I said, not understanding his point.

'Were you also aware she is located on the 21st floor?'

In the midst of laughter and the bell still ringing, I sat down fairly sharpish and tried to cover up my blushing face with minimal success. From hero to zero in a matter of seconds.

Door-to-Door Sales

In my second year at university, I decided to sell newspaper subscriptions door to door. The commission was great, and I did it in the summer so I got to work outside. I was based in Manchester and, not knowing the area, was given Moss Side as my patch.

Excited and desperate for cash, I went out to Moss Side and began door-knocking. I was aware from the look of properties that it wasn't an affluent area and I was unlikely to get offers for tea and cakes, but I wasn't here to make friends, I was here to earn cash. I was knocking away, yet was not getting anyone come to the door.

Finally, someone came to the door and it took about three minutes for them to open all the locks. Someone would have thought it was the Royal Mint. When the door finally opened, it was a gentleman wearing a white vest and boxer shorts, and he had a shaven head. He was clearly busy, as he got straight to the point.

'What do you want?', he asked. I said, 'I am here to offer you a fantastic offer we are running with the *Manchester Evening News*, where you get a one year subscription for the price of just six months'.

'Not interested', he retorted.

'Sure, you are', I said with a big grin on my face. 'You can't afford not to take this deal'.

'Are you taking the piss?', he asked.

'Of course not, you look like the sort of guy who reads the *Manchester Evening News*, and you also look the like of sort of intelligent person who wouldn't turn down a good deal when he sees one'.

'Okay', he says, 'Let me get my cheque book. Bear with me one minute'. He gently closed the door behind him.

Result, I thought. All my lines worked, and I was born to sell. As the door opened, I was expecting to take a cheque and get him to sign the form I had taken out and filled it out half. Instead, I was faced with this rather ugly dog that looked like it had rabies.

The gentleman said, 'I'm going to give you a ten-second head start, and then I'm going to unleash Duke on you'.

'What about the papers?', I asked.

Before he threw Duke at me, I just ran, faster than Usain Bolt on an off day.

32
Conclusion

'It's not the load that breaks you down, it's the way you carry it'.

—Lou Holtz

Well, I hope you have enjoyed the read and taken some tips and techniques that you can put straight into practice.

Please remember one fact that will never ever change in sales – 'people buy people first'. So you may have every sales technique in the book, but if a person doesn't like you, then it's very unlikely they will buy from you, and they certainly won't recommend you. So, be yourself and never try and copy someone else's style, as this will become very obvious to the prospect and is very off-putting. There is no harm in trying to copy someone's technique, as long as you wrap it around your own style and personality.

Sales is one of the most enjoyable and satisfying careers, and we never stop learning. No prospect or situation is ever identical, and therefore you have to adapt to every given situation. If you treat it like a game, you will start to enjoy it, and the better you get at the game, the better the rewards.

When you look at some of the greatest salespeople that have ever lived, such as Brian Tracy, Dale Carnegie and Zig Ziglar, remember they had to start somewhere. They didn't pick up the phone and close everyone they ever spoke to. They didn't win every deal in which they were involved, and they didn't build rapport with every single person they met. But one thing is guaranteed, they never gave up. They kept on learning, they set goals and they remained focused on what they wanted to achieve.

'Every winner was once a beginner'.

If you really believe that 'anything is possible', then it will be. If you asked me 15 years ago if I would have delivered sales training to over 36,000 sales professionals, written five sales books, got married to the girl of my dreams and had two beautiful children, I would have laughed at you. I have accomplished all of those things, and more, and am so excited by the prospect of more wonderful things to come further down the road in my journey.

Many people say, 'Knowledge is power'. I challenge this idea. I sincerely hope your knowledge has increased, as a result of reading this book. However, if you do nothing with that knowledge, then it's not very powerful. I believe that the implementation of knowledge is power.

Start preparing for your next week at work, set yourself goals that *you* want to achieve for the next 12 months and be as good as you allow yourself to be.

Complimentary Resources

S can the following QR Code to receive Tony's weekly
sales tips and lots more:

Tony Morris International

TONY MORRIS INTERNATIONAL

Tony Morris International delivers bespoke training courses around your business and team's needs.

Whether your team sells over the phone, face-to-face or is involved in presentations, we will have a course that is right for you. All our experts have over 15 years of experience in selling, managing salespeople and training. With over 320 clients in over 70 industries, we have a wealth of experience that we can bring to the table to add value to your business.

We have successfully helped the likes of IHG, Oakley sunglasses, Wren kitchens and many more.

When we talk about how good we are, it's showing off but when our clients do it's the proof

'Tony Morris has just spoken at our conference and he has left everybody absolutely speechless, stepping everything up a gear'.

Michaela Sams, Strategic Projects Manager at Lovelle Estate Agency

'Our conversion rate has gone from 60% to 80% overnight, cannot recommend Tony enough'.

Rob Price, Managing Director at Homes

'His presentation was the highlight of our conference'.

Toby Limerick, MD at Network Auctions

'Tony delivered a sales talk at our sales kick off conference. The audience loved him, and I thought that he was one of the best speakers I had ever seen; and I've seen hundreds. He managed to create the perfect blend of humour, practical takeaways and storytelling. I would highly recommend Tony for any sales conference'.

Jamie Paige, Partners Director at Vitality

'I was absolutely blown away by Tony's Charisma, his ability to hold an audience and his attention to detail'.

Will Polston at Evolve Mastermind

'Interesting and relevant content, delivered in an extremely eloquent, articulate and humorous manner; scored 10/10 on all four areas'.

Kari Sweet, Head of Sales effectiveness, IHG

'The way that Tony delivers is excellent and keeps everyone engaged. It is theoretical and practical, people leave with stuff that they can work on'.

Nathan Farrugia, Founder & CEO of UP–Insights, Coaching, Training

'Tony captured the sense of our company and what we are trying to do, perfectly. That's why we have booked him for our last three sales conferences'.

Christian Bo Nissen, Event Coordinator at Universal Robots

Mention of Studies or Research

In the 1960s, there was a study carried out by Dr Mehrabian and Dr Argyle on how do people communicate, Page 72.

Book Mentions

References

I love sales books. Below are some of those that have been key influences in this book and all are recommended reading.

Kerry L. Johnson (1994). *Selling with NLP: Revolutionary New Techniques That Will Double Your Sales Volume*. Nicholas Brealey.

Neil Rackham (1988). *Spin Selling*. McGraw-Hill.

Art Sobczak (1995). *How to Sell More, in Less Time, With No Rejection: Using Common Sense Telephone Techniques, Volume 1*. Business by phone.

Jeffrey Gittomer (1994). *The Sales Bible: The Ultimate Sales Resource*. Wiley.

Sean McPheat (2011). *E-Selling: The Alternative Way to Prospect and Sell for Sales Professionals: How to Use the Internet for Prospecting, Personal Branding, Networking and for Engaging the C-Suite Decision Maker*. Troubador Publishing Ltd.

Richard Denny. *Daily Quotes*.

Jeffrey Gittomer. Weekly Sales Caffeine.

www.businessballs.com

Rhonda Byrne (2006). *The Secret*. Atria Books/ Beyond Words.

Book Mentions

Bob Burg. *Go Giver* (Page 27).
Paul McGee. *SUMO* (Page 38).
Neil Rackham. *Spin Selling* (Page 67).
Dr Robert Cialdini. *Influence* (Page 73).
Rhonda Byrne. *The Secret* (Page 93).
Kerry L. Johnson (the professional tennis player). *Selling with NLP* (Neuro Linguistic Programming) (Page 224).
Dr Steve Peters. *The Chimp Paradox* (Page 35).
Art Sobczak. *Smart Calling* (Page 147).
Matthew Syed. *Bounce* (Page 294).

Index

Index

Index

Index

Index

Index

Index

Index